Small Business Finance

Small Business Finance

Rick Nason, PhD, CFA

Dan Nordqvist, CPA, CMA, MBA, MSc

BUSINESS EXPERT PRESS
Leader in applied, concise business books

First published in 2021 by
Business Expert Press, LLC
222 East 46th Street, New York, NY 10017
www.businessexpertpress.com

ISBN-13: 978-1-95253-812-4 (paperback)
ISBN-13: 978-1-95253-813-1 (e-book)

Business Expert Press Finance and Financial Management Collection

Collection ISSN: 2331-0049 (print)
Collection ISSN: 2331-0057 (electronic)

Cover image licensed by Ingram Image, StockPhotoSecrets.com
Cover and interior design by S4Carlisle Publishing Services Private Ltd., Chennai, India

First edition: 2021

10 9 8 7 6 5 4 3 2 1

Printed in the United States of America.

Abstract

According to the U.S. Small Business Administration, over 99 percent of businesses are small or medium size yet the majority of books are focused on large corporations. This book aims to close that gap and also focus on the practitioners—the entrepreneurs, small business owners, consultants—and students aspiring to practice in this space.

Small businesses are the growth engine of the economy and it is important that we provide them with the tools for success. This book covers the financial aspects of a business, including those that are important to start, grow, and sustain an enterprise. We accomplish this by providing concepts, tools, and techniques that are important for the practitioner. The overall aim is to provide this information in straightforward way while also providing the depth required for areas that warrant it.

Keywords

small business finance; entrepreneurial finance; financial statements; discounted cash flow; time value of money; financial management; financing; capital budgeting; working capital management; risk management; business valuations; pricing; venture capital

Brief Contents

Acknowledgments

Over the years we have had the opportunity to collaborate with some amazing individuals and businesses who work tirelessly in the small business space. They are the backbone of our economy and this book is dedicated to them.

We want to thank our respective families for their patience as we have spent many hours away from them to make this book a reality.

CHAPTER 1

The Small Business Difference

Small businesses, whether they be sole proprietors, partnerships, family businesses, entrepreneurial ventures, or an innovator trying to challenge the current business status quo, all play an important part in the economy. Although it is the giant multinational corporations that seem to be the focus of attention, it is small businesses that drive the global economy.

There is a romantic sentiment to small businesses. The oft-repeated story of the origins of the giant Apple that started out as three friends starting out in their garage to create one of the world's greatest and most innovative companies. Before that there was Henry Ford, working away as a sole proprietor trying to create a car for the masses. In virtually every industry, the story gets repeated of a business owner starting with limited resources but unlimited dreams to create a business that became a household name for generations.

The reality is however that most small businesses remain small. They may remain small for a variety of reasons, including lack of scope or scalability, lack of ambition or vision of the founders to expand beyond their existing base, contentedness of owners with current scope of operations, insufficient financing, being limited by competitive businesses, and lack of skill to exploit an opportunity.

This book is written explicitly for the small business owner and operator or those who desire to create and start their own small business. Small businesses obviously share many traits with their more notable big cousins, the publicly traded company or the large privately owned firm. However, small businesses also have many separate operating principles that are quite distinct from those of their larger relatives. This is especially so in the area of financial management.

In this chapter we begin by examining the importance of small businesses to the overall U.S. economy. Small businesses make up 99.9 percent of all businesses and 65 percent of net new jobs in the United States.[1] They generate 44 percent of GDP and 48 percent of employment.[2] These numbers attest that the cumulative importance of small businesses on the national economy is indeed very significant. The chapter continues to examine what makes small businesses special when it comes to the financial management of the business. Small businesses have more than just size to differentiate them. Their mode of operations is also a significant differentiating factor, and the differentiating financial factors are the reason for this book.

The Small Business Market

For our purposes, a small business is one that does not have publicly traded financial assets, such as stock or bonds, nor does it have institutionalized and syndicated bank loans. Although this still leaves the possibility of some very large private firms, our focus is on firms that have assets ranging from zero up to approximately five million dollars. Definitions for what constitutes a small business tend to vary widely by country or even by region. We are not going to concern ourselves with an exact definition but leave it up to the common sense and intuition of the reader.

A small business could consist of a single proprietor operating out of the basement of their home or an operation with over 100 employees with one or more manufacturing facilities. It could be a partnership providing professional services, an entrepreneur developing a new medical device or app, a seasoned professional who retired earlier to earn from their expertise as a consultant, an artist selling their art on the Internet, or a family business that has been in continuous operation for over a 100 years.

Small businesses exist in every industry and provide or produce every conceivable type of product or service. While most are highly specialized

---

[1]U.S. Small Business Administration Office of Advocacy. September, 2019. "What's New with Small Business."

[2]U.S. Small Business Administration Office of Advocacy. December, 2018. "Small Business GDP 1998–2014."

in what they do, some may offer a portfolio of services. What is unique about small businesses is that they are operated for the purposes and benefits of their owner and operators, rather than for the somewhat impersonal legal entity that constitutes the large corporation.

Small businesses are a very significant part of the economy, not just in North America but around the world. Figure 1.1 shows how critical small businesses are to employment around the globe.

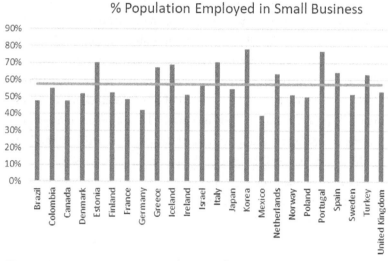

Figure 1.1 Small business employment[3]

The First Small Business Difference: Business Objectives

Small businesses differ in many ways from large corporations. These differences are what make small businesses so attractive to so many investors and entrepreneurs who wish to develop their own small business rather than work in a probably more stable and less risky large corporation. As previously mentioned, small businesses are run for the benefit of their owners and operators, rather than for the financial stakeholders, which is the case for larger corporations.

---

[3]OECD Data. SDBS Structural Business Statistics-ISIC4. Business Statistics by Employment Size Class. 1-249 persons employed (SMEs).

This brings us to the first and primary difference in the financial management of a small business, namely, that of objectives. Every student of business or business law learns that the goal of a publicly traded company is to maximize shareholder wealth.[4] This is accomplished by maximizing the return on investment for the risk involved in the investments. Maximize shareholder wealth is a central tenet, if not *the* central tenet, of corporate finance. Conversely, maximize shareholder wealth is frequently *not* the central tenet of a small business.

One of the significant advantages of using shareholder wealth maximization as an operating objective is that it is objective and relatively easy to calculate. For publicly traded companies, they can observe their stock price on a daily real-time basis. While stock prices contain a large amount of noise, the reality is that over a period of time, the stock price provides a fair and reasonable assessment of how well the organization is doing. However, stock price, and its associated corporate objective of maximizing shareholder value, is extremely myopic and limiting in scope.

Maximizing shareholder value does not take into account the many nonfinancial objectives that stakeholders may wish to take into account. Issues such as sustainability, social good, and other possible objectives do not easily fit within the confines of maximizing shareholder wealth. Likewise, these alternative objectives are not as simple to measure or to observe.

The small business owner, while certainly concerned about return and risk on their investment, is likely to have several different and more important (to them at least) objectives that they are operating under. For many small business operators, it is likely known to them that the probability is quite high that they would be better off at maximizing their own wealth by working for a large corporation. Yet they choose to put their own wealth at risk by working in small business so they can satisfy other, more important goals and objectives.

One of the objectives that the small business owner may be seeking is freedom—freedom to operate a business in the manner that they choose, freedom to make independent decisions, freedom to work flexible hours

---

[4] There is also a relatively new type of corporation called a Benefit Corporation. It is a form of incorporation that explicitly includes social and environmental goals in addition to the profit-making goal as articles of their incorporation.

(despite the demanding hours required of a small business operator), or a host of other freedoms that operating a small business gives one.

Like many nonfinancial objectives, it is difficult, if not impossible, to put a price on freedom. Additionally, freedom is a highly subjective value. To one person, the freedom of operating a small business may bring a lot of pleasures, while to a different person the pressures of having to make and be responsible for decisions may be a source of unpleasant pressures.

In line with the freedom objective, there is personal accountability to account for in the management of a small business. A small business owner may be directly responsible for the incomes of their employees, to say nothing of their own financial well-being. This sense of personal accountability can be a strong motivator for some small business operators, who derive a great deal of personal satisfaction from knowing that they "did it their way."

For a family business, the financial objectives may extend well beyond that of current employees and extend to family members that depend on financial dividends from the firm in order to maintain their lifestyles. An additional consideration with the family firm is that of stewardship. No one wants to be the family manager of the family firm that sends the firm into bankruptcy or has to close the business due to inept management practices. This sense of stewardship and the family conflicts that may ensue present a special consideration of the trade-offs in setting the objectives for the firm.

Many owner-operator businesses were created to bring a passion of the owner to others. This passion could have revolved around a sport, a hobby, or a passion to provide a special service to the community. These businesses are generally not maximizing financial returns for the owner (although some are and are very profitable), but the joy of running the business around a passion has its own set of different rewards to offer.

Some small businesses are set up by entrepreneurs who have few other options. For a variety of reasons working in a corporate office may not be feasible, or other constraints, such as family commitments, may be limiting their income producing activities. Developing and operating their own business may be simply the last resort for earning income.

Finally, we are experiencing a trend of small businesses being operated by managers who have running a small business as an aspirational goal, or a "bucket-list" item if you will. For these individuals, operating a small business has been an objective for a period of time and they are implementing their wish.

The point is that each small business likely has objectives and reasons for existing that extend well beyond that of simply minimizing risk and maximizing returns. There is a plethora of objectives beyond maximizing shareholder wealth for the small business owner. This makes the financial management challenge less dogmatic and more subtle. What is optimal in normal financial practice may not be optimal for every small business owner. This is a point that needs to be kept in mind when reading through this book.

As an example of how these objectives differ, we will consider an example from Chapter 7 on working capital management. In Chapter 7 we argue that a company will likely not want to keep an excessive amount of cash in the company bank account as there will likely be better uses for the money than sitting idle. In light of this we recommend that to avoid carrying excess cash, the small business should instead take occasional advantage of short-term financing, such as an operating loan from a bank. This is great advice if the firm wishes to be most efficient with its resources. However, if the small business owner is adverse to any form of external financing, and if in addition they are extremely risk adverse, then by all means they should ignore our advice on that point and do what they believe is in their best interest.

The difference in objectives is the beauty of operating a small business. You get to decide what is important to you, the owner-manager, and you get to decide what strategies help you best accomplish your objectives. This difference in objectives is not a weakness, but a strength that gives small businesses their own individual personalities.

Triple Bottom Line

A specific example of alternative motives for small businesses is the operating philosophy known as Triple Bottom Line. The Triple Bottom Line objectives, often loosely referred to as People, Planet, and Profits, attempt to incorporate objectives beyond shareholder wealth. The Triple Bottom

Line attempts to incorporate not only economic factors into decision making, but also societal and environmental factors.

The Triple Bottom Line has a lot of attractive qualities to it. It is constructed to be a socially responsible business, which of course is attractive to not only consumers but also to business owners and the people who work in such businesses. However, there are issues with measuring the objectives, which are often at odds with each other.

As an example of the measurement and trade-off issues with using a Triple Bottom Line methodology, consider the case of a pulp mill in an economically depressed town that has high unemployment. A proposed expansion of the pulp mill would be positive for the economic profits of the mill's owners, and it would be a boom to the employment and payrolls of the depressed area. However, a larger pulp mill would generally be considered quite harmful to the environment. Thus, there are conflicting trade-offs between employment, economics, and the environment. There are also resulting measurement issues. For example, how to determine the tradeoff between pollution caused by economic expansion versus the jobs gained and the collective self-esteem boost that comes from getting people off welfare and gainfully employed? There are no easy answers for such questions, and while our pulp mill example is very specific to a large corporation, it is almost certainly the case that a small business owner adopting Triple Bottom Line would face similar, if smaller scale dilemmas.

For many businesspeople, the difficulties of strictly trying to maximize three somewhat conflicting sets of objectives are offset by the benefits of building a socially responsible business. Thus, one of the trends in small businesses is those that are being started for Triple Bottom Line reasons. There is a growing trend of entrepreneurs who are starting businesses with this alternative model. For instance, many coffee and small fast-food restaurants are capitalizing on the desire for consumers to have ethically sourced products. Thus, we see "Fair Trade" coffee shops that only source coffee beans from suppliers who pay a fair price for the beans to coffee growers and coffee pickers. Another example is food shops that operate on a 100-mile basis that only source food that is grown within a 100-mile radius to cut down on the environmental effects of packaging and shipping.

The Second Small Business Difference: Risk

A second major way small businesses differ from their larger cousins in terms of their risk management. Small businesses differ in their capabilities to manage risk. They also have a much wider set of attitudes toward risk. We will begin by discussing the differences in ability to manage risk.

There are three significant ways in which the ability of a small business to manage differs from that of larger companies: capital and operational constraints, inability to build a portfolio of strategies, and their flexibility. Publicly traded companies, and even large privately owned companies, have a much wider array of financing opportunities than your typical small business does. Access to capital is one of the main risk reduction strategies. Admittedly, taking advantage of too much access to capital can lead to overleverage and bankruptcy. On the whole however access to capital allows a business to more easily manage during the inevitable peaks and troughs of business activity that will be experienced.

Due to constrained resources, small businesses generally cannot attract the type or quantity of specialist managers. For instance, few, if any, small businesses have a dedicated team of managers to deal with risk management issues or cybersecurity issues. By contrast, most publicly traded corporations will have a dedicated team of highly trained professionals for each of these managerial components. The irony of course is that risk management and cybersecurity are probably more important to the small business owner than they are to the large corporation.

The capital and operational constraints also manifest themselves in the portfolio of products and services that the business offers. Portfolio diversification is a cornerstone of maximizing return while minimizing risk. Think of three separate shops: One sells only umbrellas, one sells only sunglasses, and one sells both umbrellas and sunglasses. The shop that sells both umbrellas and sunglasses will prosper in all types of weather, while the specialty shops will go through times of boom and bust. In terms of return and risk management, this simple example illustrates that it is preferable to have a portfolio of products and services.

The reality for most small businesses however is that they need to focus on a small, and generally undiversified, set of products and services due to constraints in resources. Thus, a shop that sells umbrellas might expand to also sell raincoats, but this provides only a little bit of diversification and does not help the business during long sunny periods. It is not only in products and services for offer that small business are hampered by a lack of diversification. It is also in terms of strategies and markets that they go after. A small business needs to stay focused, on a small set of strategies and a small set of markets. This is great if they choose the right strategies and they choose the right markets to focus on, but it is potentially disastrous if they choose incorrectly or even just encounter a period of bad luck or a poor economic cycle.

This brings us to the third characteristic of a small business regarding risk, and that is their flexibility. A small business generally has much more flexibility to change strategy and tactics than a much larger, publicly traded company does. The flexibility can be a positive or a negative, but the astute small business operator will leverage flexibility to great advantage when necessary.

A whole branch of thinking, popularly called "Starting Lean," has arisen in the small business literature.[5] In essence, a starting lean strategy says that a small business should develop products and services as quickly as possible and get them to market and then let the marketplace illustrate to the business owner how to develop and improve their product. This is opposed to the more traditional thinking of building the best product possible before going to market with it. The starting lean philosophy is leveraging the ability of small businesses to be flexible in their strategies (or to use the trendy term "pivot") and thus make up for their resource constraints by being nimbler.

The flexibility of the small business applies not only to strategies and operating modes, but also to financial strategies and tactics. Although financing opportunities for small businesses are generally limited, and the range of financial strategies that a small business can reasonably employ is also limited, a small business as a general rule should build more flexibility into their financial strategies, all else being equal, than their bigger, more diversified publicly traded cousins might.

---

[5]See E. Reis. 2011. *The Lean Startup: How Today's Entrepreneurs Use Continuous Innovation to Create Radically Successful Businesses* (New York, NY: Currency), for a description of the starting lean operating philosophy.

Not only do small businesses differ in their capabilities for managing risk, but they also differ in their attitudes toward risk. In part, this difference in attitude stems from the difference in operating objectives that we talked about previously in this chapter. However, it also differs in that small business owners tend to have much more diverse risk appetites and risk attitudes than are generally seen among typical large corporations.

In general, small businesses tend to take on significantly higher levels of risk. Part of this may be due to ignorance about risk and risk management (which we aim to remedy in Chapter 10), and part of this is likely attributable to the naturally higher risk tolerances of small business owners.

The risk attitudes of small business owners are also shaped much more by their stakeholders than it would be for the manager of a large corporation. In a publicly traded organization, the manager has almost zero direct contact with the shareholders of the corporation. Even the board members have extremely limited contact with the vast majority of shareholders. In contrast, a small business owner most likely has a very clear knowledge of each and every one of their financial stakeholders—both the explicit stakeholders and the implicit stakeholders.

The lack of anonymity of stakeholders instills the small business manager with a different risk attitude. It is no longer a faceless (and assumed greedy) stockholder, but likely a family friend, or even a family member. If the business performs poorly, then this reflects on the social standing among the group of friends of the small business operator. This makes risk a part of a social construct.

Even if the business is totally self-financed, this has risk implications as well. First, there may be dependents, such as offspring, who rely on the operator for their financial well-being. Second, the fact that it is not only the reputation, but also the finances, of the small business manager at risk makes risk personal and very different from the risk attitude of an employee working at a publicly traded organization.

Therefore, the risk attitudes of operating a small business are very different in nature than the risk attitudes of a corporation. The reality is that the variability of returns, or the risk, of operating a small business is much greater. This exacerbates the fact that the personal and social attitudes toward risk are also much greater. This combination means that the individual attitudes toward risk taking of the small business owner anecdotally tend to be quite different from that of a corporately employed business manager.

Small business managers need to think about financing and financial management differently due to the need to think about risk differently. Ultimately, financial management is about risk and return. It is about how risk and return determine the financing of the business; it is about how risk and return determine the operating strategies; it is about how risk and return determine the marketing approach; and most of all it is about how risk and return determine the financial strategy and tactics. These differences, combined with the differences in sources of financing (the subject of the next section), are why a specific book for financial management for small business needs to be written.

The Third Small Business Difference: Financing Sources

Financing sources for a small business will be covered in depth in Chapter 6, but it is useful to introduce some of the issues here as financing is the third major difference in operating a small business. A publicly traded corporation, by definition, issues publicly traded shares, and generally also publicly traded debt. The public exchange markets work wonders for large-scale capitalism. However, the characteristics that create their efficiency at raising large sums of capital for large businesses are also the characteristics that make them ill-suited as sources of financing for small business. Thus, the last category of the small business difference is sources of financing.

A small business generally goes through a series of stages, with each stage having a different set of financing alternatives. There is generally a start-up phase, a build and grow phase, and then a maturity phase. There may also be a blossoming into a public company stage for those businesses that have both the ability and the desire to do so.

During the initial start-up phase, funding generally comes from two sources: individual, or self-financing, and family and friends. Both of these sources of financing are obvious and commonly used. The reasons for their use is that they are often the only form of initial financing available. Most other sources of financing are not available until there is an initial proof of concept prototype, or at least a feasible business plan in place. The issue is that it takes resources in time, managerial expertise, and money to even get to this stage.

What is not evident about self-financing or financing from friends and family is the cost of such financing. Many entrepreneurs think that self-financing is free. It is anything but! Self-financing or financing from friends and family are very expensive options when you examine the level of risk. The only aspect that makes self-financing at all practical is that the amounts involved are generally relatively small. The risk of losing everything however is great.

When considering the cost of start-up financing, the entrepreneur should consider what return they would be earning on their financial investment if they invested in equivalently risky assets. As a benchmark, consider a professional venture capitalist, a financier that we will discuss later in this section. Typically, a venture capitalist must calculate an expected return of at least 25 percent before they will consider making an investment, and they only invest much later in the process after the concept has been proven and the risk level is much lower!

The other cost that is often ignored is the cost of the time of the entrepreneur. There is a cost in terms of the time spent, there is a cost in terms of the energy expended, and there is an opportunity cost in terms of foregone income that could have been achieved from working for an existing company.

In the context of the risks, and in the context of the real costs, the total cost of self-financing or financing from friends or family is very real and very significant. This is even before considering the unseen, but the very real cost of the stress involved with being responsible for the trust shown in the business by family and friends. If traditional financial analysis techniques were used to decide whether or not someone should start a business, then very few business plans would survive the analysis and very few businesses would be started. Fortunately, that doesn't happen, and that is why we need to think about risk and return differently for small businesses.

The next stage is the growth stage of the business. Here we are assuming that the business has developed an early form of the product or service, and there is at least a glimmer of hope that the business might be successful. In addition to a continuation of self-financing and financing from friends and family, a host of other sources come into play.

A traditional additional source of financing at this stage is an Angel Investor. An Angel Investor is generally a wealthy individual (although it could be a special purpose fund) who invests in very early stage companies. The Angel Investor will generally offer a combination of financing in the sense of a loan at preferred interest as well as equity in which they take an ownership stake in the business. An Angel Investor generally builds a portfolio composed of a relatively large number of these very early stage companies in which they have (for them) a relatively small investment. In addition to providing financing, some, not all, Angel Investors will also provide some business coaching or make introductions for the business. In this sense, an Angel Investor is like a very early stage Venture Capitalist.

Another important source of financing at this stage is government sponsored programs. Given the importance of small business to the overall economy, the government has an incentive to have as many as possible small businesses go through the start-up to growth phase. There are a variety of both local, state as well as national programs to assist in securing such financing.[6] In addition, many of the government programs also provide some form of development training and coaching.

A unique form of financing for early stage companies has developed in the last decade. Earlier we talked about how the major stock exchanges are effective for raising large sums of money for publicly traded corporations but inefficient for small businesses. Various ventures however have utilized the capabilities of the Internet to use similar principles as the public exchanges to develop a form of financing known as "crowdfunding." With crowdfunding, the company seeks small investments from a large number of potential investors. The investors are procured through a crowdfunding exchange set up by one of many different companies on the Internet. The efficiency of the Internet, and the ability to connect with a large number of global Internet users, makes crowdfunding a

---

[6]U.S. Small Business Administration Funding Programs. https://www.sba.gov/funding-programs; Grants.gov. https://www.grants.gov/web/grants/home.html; The Small Business Innovation Research (SBIR) program. https://www.sbir.gov/.

viable alternative. In effect, a crowdfunding investor is like a typical stock or bond investor, except that the amounts being invested are very small compared with traditional investments, and the regulatory framework is much less stringent. The ability of everyone to connect to the Internet is what makes crowdfunding feasible.

There are significant advantages and disadvantages of crowdfunding. The advantage for the small business owner is that it is a relatively accessible form of early stage financing, and it gets the concept of the company into the public's attention. The downside is that it is a highly unregulated market (although that may soon change), and thus issues, such as property rights, may be difficult to enforce. While crowdfunding is still in the early stages of development as a small business financing avenue, the early success of the methodology suggests that it will be around for a while.

Once the company has developed a business plan and a working prototype, it may consider joining a business incubator, also known as a business accelerator. A business incubator is an organization that exists to bring similar early growth stage companies together to share resources such as office space, receptionists, and office machines, such as copiers and printers. They also provide business coaching and introductions to a variety of potential investors. Some incubators are for-profit and will command a fee or an equity position in the business, while not-for-profit incubators are run as part of research or governmental programs.

Several incubators have become well known for nurturing and producing highly successful companies or "graduates." Competition to be selected for such well-known incubators is extremely high. Applicants to such programs need to have a well-formed model business model in order to have their application successful.

Once a company has developed itself, it can start to seek more traditional modes of financing, including bank financing and bootstrapping. Banks are generally quite reluctant to lend to early stage companies due to the level of risk. However, once a company establishes a steady cash flow stream, the banks will be more willing to consider financing and offer a variety of forms of financing. Of course, once a company has a steady cash flow stream, it can consider bootstrapping itself, using the proceeds from sales to finance future sales.

If the company wants to expand further, and potentially go on to become a publicly listed company, then that is when venture capital becomes relevant. A venture capital company raises money from investors for the specific purpose of investing in early stage companies. Generally, a venture capitalist is not interested in small businesses per se. A venture capitalist invests almost exclusively in companies that have the potential to eventually become publicly traded. Therefore, venture capital financing is relatively late stage financing, and by the time a venture capitalist becomes involved, the company has already gone through several rounds of financing and has a marketable product for a period of time. In fact, once a venture capitalist become involved, the company is likely on the edge of no longer being considered a small business.

Financing for a small business is as much of a journey as it is anything else. There are stages of financing that correspond to the stages of the business as it grows. The unique elements of financing a small business are another of the distinguishing features that make small business finance unique.

Concluding Thoughts

The vast bulk of what passes for best practice in business finance is based on the large corporate model. This is unfortunate. First, small businesses are a very important part of the economy and an important driver of growth. Second, small businesses operate very different from their publicly traded peers and the principles of best financial practice are thus quite different.

In this chapter we have discussed three of the critical characteristics driving these differences. The first is that small businesses often have very different objectives and priorities than the simple "maximize wealth" that publicly traded corporations follow. Small business owners and operators manage their businesses to a variety of objectives that may be as unique as their business.

A second major difference is that small businesses operate on very different principles of risk. Small businesses do not have the luxury of having natural risk diversification through scale of products, scope, or geographical diversification. In fact, most small businesses have almost no diversification, which dramatically challenges their risk profile.

The third major difference is the range of financing alternatives available to the small business. A small business does not have the luxury of issuing shares or debt to the general investing public. Securing a single source of financing is often a major struggle for small businesses, much less trying to optimally select from among many sources.

The remaining chapters of this book go through the concepts and ideas of best practice as specifically applied to small business. Admittedly, small business finance is often as much of an art as it is a science. Our hope is that this book provides some guidance and helps improve the financial decision making of the small business owner or operator.

CHAPTER 2

Nine Small Business Finance Concepts

In this chapter we want to lay out a few general principles and dispel a few myths. Much of this material may seem obvious, but our experience tells us that much of it is sadly ignored, never learned, or forgotten. Additionally, some of it goes against the grain of what is considered conventional finance knowledge or is considered to be counterintuitive. However, that should be expected, as we believe, and think that you should also appreciate that financial management for small business is not the same as financial management for the publicly traded corporation.

The nine small business financial concepts discussed in this short chapter are as follows:

- The financial strategy exists solely to support business objectives
- Capital is an asset
- Cash and cash flow rule
- A dollar today is worth more than a dollar tomorrow
- Risk is not what you think it is
- Finance is the management of risk and return
- Ideas should chase money; money should never chase ideas
- Financial risk should complement business risk
- The goal of the manager is to maximize utility, not wealth

We will continually refer back to these ideas throughout the book. Let's get started.

The Financial Strategy Exists Solely to
Support Business Objectives

Whatever the financial strategy, it should exist to support the growth and sustainability of the business. This seems so obvious as to not be worth saying. The sad reality however is that for many businesses, both large and small, it seems that the business is run more for financial reasons than for business reasons.

It is quite true that having and implementing a prudent financial strategy can significantly add value to a business. However, if the sole value added from the business comes from the financing strategy, then it is not a business at all but simply a financial trading scheme.

Whatever we, or any other financial consultants may recommend, it should be checked against the objectives of the business as well as the objectives of the business owners. A simple as well as very common example is in the use of debt. Later in this section we will suggest that financial risk (the use of debt and leverage) should be increased for a business that has stable and predictable positive cash flows. This is a well-known adage of financial professionals. However, a primary objective of the business owner might have been to develop for themselves an ultra-low-stress source of income. Furthermore, they may have moral or religious attitudes toward the use of debt and leverage. To this we claim that the desires and wishes of the business owner trump best financial practice.

A more serious case is when the financial strategy is driving business strategy. Consider, for example, a case of government incentives to expand a business. While government sponsored and discounted financing is obviously something that should prudently be taken advantage of, it also should not be the sole reason for the expansion. If the expansion does not make sense for business purposes, then it will not in the long term make sense no matter how good the financial incentives are.

A brilliantly implemented financial strategy cannot and will not, in the long run, save a faulty business strategy. The financial strategy exists to support the business strategy, and not the other way around.

Capital Is an Asset

This seems like an obvious and needless statement. "Of course, capital is an asset," you are thinking, but are you truly thinking about capital as an asset? There are many assets of a business: Managerial time, human resources, machines, any proprietary knowledge, passion of managers and employees, and loyal customers are just some of the most important assets. The asset that underlies all of these other assets, and the one asset that is likely the most highly constrained, is capital. Capital allows for the purchase of, and investment in, almost every other asset with the exception of passion. Even then, if capital constraints lead to financial stress, then even the passion of the managers and employees will likely be tested beyond their endurance.

In Chapter 4 we will discuss many different metrics, including measuring the efficiency of capital. Understanding the drivers of return on capital employed is one of the most critical tasks for continued success of a small business. With limited alternatives for financing, especially when compared with the greater financing alternatives for publicly traded organizations, a small business needs to make sure that its capital is working most efficiently for itself and its business objectives.

Measuring capital efficiency is relatively easy for a publicly traded corporation; it can most appropriately be measured by stock price returns or more directly by calculating a return on capital employed ratio (which again, will be covered in Chapter 4). For a small business the measurement of capital efficiency may be much more nuanced given the many objectives of a small business that likely go well beyond simply financial success or maximizing wealth—a topic that is more fully discussed in the last section of this chapter. If the objectives of the business include nonfinancial objectives, such as lifestyle flexibility or following a passion, then capital asset efficiency needs rethinking.

Cash and Cash Flow Rule

Many people think that profits or returns are the goal of a business. The reality is that successful businesses focus on cash and cash flow. More simply, the cash and cash flow rule! While profits and positive returns are nice, the reality is that you cannot purchase supplies with profits or accounting returns nor can you pay employees or even yourself with profits or returns. Cash and cash flow are what is required to grow (or even just maintain) the business, ensure its survival, and pay benefits to managers, employees as well as all of the other stakeholders.

Admittedly it is *positive* cash flow that matters. The cash flow coming in must exceed the cash flow going out. Positive cash flow sounds a lot like profits, but the two are very different. While this is a topic that will be explained more fully in Chapters 3 and 4, for now it suffices to acknowledge that accounting conventions include a lot of transactions that do not involve cash or cash flow. These accounting assumptions can lead to incorrect conclusions being made about the success of a business and to faulty decision making.

Take the simple example of selling to a significant customer who is always very tardy in paying their invoices. From the accounting point of view selling to this customer may be quite profitable. However, if the fact is acknowledged that expenses need to be paid for and financed while waiting for this customer to pay their own invoice, it will reveal that selling to this customer may have very little profit involved and indeed may mean you are selling to them at a loss. The accounting bottom line looks great, but the negative cash flows that build while waiting for the delinquent customer to pay their invoices may be bankrupting the company.

In Chapter 4, we discuss various metrics for examining the cash flows of a company. The most important is the Statement of Cash Flows. The Statement of Cash Flows breaks down the cash inflows and outflows of the Income Statement and Balance Sheet into three categories: Operating Activities, Investment Activities, and Financing Activities. Due to a focus on profits instead of cash flows, the company may have positive Net Income yet have negative Operating Cash Flows (cash flows from making things and selling things). The importance of these negative Operating Cash Flows may be disguised by positive cash flows from Financing Activities or Investing Activities. Admittedly a healthy business generally has cash flows from both Financing Activities and Investing Activities, but these activities should not dominate the cash flows from Operating Activities.

In the start-up phase of any business it is likely that the business will have negative cash flows, and these negative cash flows obviously need to be financed in some way. Ultimately, however, if a business does not generate positive cash flows, it will not be successful. Propping up a negative cash flow business with financing—whatever the form of financing—is not a long-term formula for success.

Many financial consultants—including us—believe that the focus on accounting profits has gone too far. Accounting serves a very valid purpose and proper accounting has aided an uncountable number of businesses to develop and thrive. However, the short termism of accounting, particularly for publicly traded corporations, has exposed some of the limitations of being profit focused.

It is absolutely critical that the manager of a small business understand the limitations of relying on accounting profits versus positive cash flows. It is necessary that the small business manager learns the strengths and disadvantages of both approaches. Ultimately though, strong accounting results (as measured by positive net income in the income statement) will not save a business that has continual negative cash flows from operations.

Accounting is going to remain a bedrock of financial management for a long time to come. However, accounting principles were developed in a different time and era of business. With the digital economy, digital cash, and the onset of fintech products, the nature of the flow of cash has started to change dramatically.

Before concluding this section, it is important at this point to realize that cash is static and cash flow is dynamic. Static cash by itself is not that useful an asset other than for the flexibility it provides due to its potential to be put to use in investment to grow the business. A large cash hoard is thus not necessarily a good thing, although it is better than a huge negative debt that has no prospects for being repaid. Thus, particularly for small businesses, who are generally cash constrained, a focus on cash flow is particularly warranted. Cash, and particularly cash flow, rules!

A Dollar Today Is Worth More Than a Dollar Tomorrow

One of the unbreakable rules of finance is that there is a time value of money; in more basic terms, a dollar today is worth more than a dollar tomorrow. This is the basis of why interest rates are almost always positive.[1]

---

[1] As we write this is in early 2020, it is true that some parts of the world do have negative interest rates that are available to large lending institutions. This is an economic distortion that has baffled economists and is a consequence of the 2008 recession and the efforts of Central Banks around the world going to sometimes extreme measures trying to stimulate their economies.

Investors and stakeholders expect, and indeed demand, a positive return on their investment in the business.

There are three main reasons why there is a time value of money. The first is inflation. As an economy grows, things become more expensive. When my wife and I just got married, we used to take advantage of a restaurant's heavily advertised special of "Two Can Dine for $7.99." We annually go back and order the same meal; the last time it cost over $28! Inflation is the most obvious of the reasons as to why there is a time value of money effect, but two other reasons may be even more important.

The second reason there is a time value of money is risk. When capital is invested, there is a risk that the capital may be lost due to bad business decisions, a bad business, or just bad luck. Not every business, whether large or small, succeeds, and no business succeeds forever. To account for the very real possibility of losing money, investors and stakeholders will rationally expect a positive return to compensate them for the negative risk that they are taking. As will be discussed later in this chapter, the greater the assumed risk, the greater the expected return will be and thus the greater the time value of money.

The third component of the time value of money is the opportunity cost involved. Cash that is tied up in an investment is not available for other uses. This may mean that special and unique opportunities may be missed. It also means that there is a reduced level of financial flexibility for the investor. The investor needs to be compensated for this opportunity cost. The longer the time period that the investment is tied up, the greater the opportunity cost and the greater the time value of money.

In Chapter 8 we will discuss how to account for this time value of money when making investment decisions by incorporating a discount factor into the analysis. The important principle to remember at this point is that there is a time value to money and the three major factors driving the time value are inflation, risk, and opportunity costs.

Risk Is Not What You Think It Is

When asked for their definition of risk, most people will respond with something like, "It is the probability that something bad will happen." This is a very limiting definition of risk, and one that is actually quite inaccurate in technical terms. In Chapter 10 we will discuss risk and risk management at length, but for now it is important to introduce a better definition of risk. That better definition of risk, and the definition of risk that we will use throughout this book is, "Risk is the possibility that bad or good things may happen."

Using our revised definition of risk is more than just a matter of semantics. It is a definition that has the potential to change the culture of a business and the way that it does business. It is a definition that is more in line with how many small business owners operate, even though they may be unaware of it. It is a definition that mitigates value-destroying beliefs about risk.

There are three components to our definition of risk: a forward-looking bias, a component of uncertainty, and a focus on both the upside and downside of risk. The first component is that of a forward-looking bias. Almost by definition, many small business operators are optimists by nature. In turn, optimists are forward looking. Entrepreneurs by necessity must be forward looking—they are attempting to create something out of nothing. Small business operators need to be forward looking as well as their flexibility and agility to adapt as circumstances change is one of their key business attributes.

Too often, we put too much emphasis on the past to inform our decisions about what must be done going forward. The past is great for learning lessons, but it does not predetermine the future. Business is dynamic and not a direct extrapolation of the past. If it was, then few new businesses would be developed, and entrepreneurship by definition would have no reason to exist. What happened in the past is known with certainty; there is no risk involved. It is only the future where we do not know what will happen, and thus risk and risk management is a forward-looking exercise.

This concept leads directly to the second element—risk involves uncertainty.[2] Risk is about the future and the future is uncertain. We may

---

[2]For academic readers it is important to point out that in certain academic classifications risk and uncertainty are two quite different things. In academic terms, risk is an event about which there is a probabilistic defined set of outcomes. For example, the roll of a dice cube where we know that one of the six sides will turn face up and the probability of each of the six sides turning up is one-sixth. Uncertainty is reserved for events in which the set of outcomes cannot be defined. For instance, we cannot predict which music performer will be most popular 50 years from now as it is likely that such a performer has not yet been born. For our purposes, these academic differences are not relevant.

make intelligent or informed guesses about the future, but ultimately no one knows what the future holds, particularly when it comes to the fortunes of a small business. The greater the range of future outcomes, and the smaller the level of confidence or knowledge about potential future outcomes, the greater the risk.

The final concept involving our definition of risk is that it involves upside as well as downside components. This component is somewhat controversial and is not part of most laypersons' concept of risk. However, it is simply a recognition that the future could turn out to be positive as well as negative. It seems only rational and prudent that the small business owner should think of risk in both terms so that they can be better prepared to mitigate downside risk as well as capture upside risk. In Chapter 10 we will expand on this to state that "risk management is managing in such a way as to increase the probability and magnitude of good risk events happening while also managing so as to decrease the probability and severity of bad risk events occurring."

Understanding the two-sided nature of risk and adopting a truer definition of risk is a significant improvement in managing risk in a small business. This is a concept that will be expanded on in Chapter 10, which discusses risk management.

Finance Is the Management of Risk and Return

Finance involves trade-offs. The most fundamental financial trade-off is that between risk and return as measured by increased positive cash flows or increased wealth and benefits. In principle, the greater the risk, the greater the expected return.

For a practical example, consider the case when making capital investments. When determining a target return from a business venture or investment, a key principle to remember is that the expected return should compensate for the amount of risk involved. A higher risk investment (e.g., in an experimental and untested piece of manufacturing equipment or an innovative product line expansion) should hold the promise of a higher expected return than the return from making a lower risk investment (e.g., an investment in an updated piece of equipment or expansion of a popular existing line of products).

You probably know the adage that states "There is no such thing as a free lunch." The same holds for finance. Benefits (in the case of a business, wealth or utility) are going to, on average, be in line with their costs. Investors will only invest (put at risk) a small amount for something that has a small expected benefit. Likewise, investors will be willing to invest (put at risk) a much larger amount for something that has a much larger expected benefit.

It has been well documented that financial assets, such as stock prices and bond prices, move in such a way so as to compensate investors according to the amount of risk that they are taking. Riskier stocks and bonds, on average, produce higher average returns for their investors; they also lead to losses a higher percentage of the time as well. It is a clear example of the principle "the greater the risk, the greater the expected return."

The small business manager should keep this general principle in mind when making business decisions. Decisions that involve higher levels of risk should also lead to expectations of higher return. Note that a higher return may or may not materialize—risk involves losses as well as gains. The key point is that the expectation should be there at the beginning of the investment.

Choosing to engage in risky business activities when the expected return is low is a formula for business failure. Chapter 8, on capital budgeting, goes into detail on how to formally incorporate this return to risk trade-off in financial decision making.

Ideas Should Chase Money; Money Should Never Chase Ideas

An old saying of prudent financial management is that "Ideas should chase money; money should not chase ideas." You can likely recall a time when you unexpectedly came into some extra money. It might, for instance, had been when you put on an old coat and discovered that you left a $100 bill in one of the pockets. Now think about what you did with such a windfall: Did you spend that surprise cash wisely or did you waste it on something frivolous? Unless you have an unusual amount of financial discipline, the odds are great that you essentially wasted the windfall. The same is true when cash goes looking for business ideas. The results of the investment are not likely to be as well thought out as when a well-structured idea goes looking for financing.

The amount of cash reserve that a business should try to maintain will be discussed later in the book. The reality of most small businesses is that they are cash constrained. This is not necessarily an issue in the normal course of a business. Of course, if the cash constraints are such that normal business activities cannot be undertaken, then that is an issue. However, as long as the cash flow is sufficient to maintain the business, pay employees, and investors, the situation should be considered to be fine. It should not necessarily be the aim of the business to stockpile excess cash, and if excess cash is somehow accrued, extra discipline should be applied in how that cash is deployed. To reiterate what was mentioned in the beginning: Ideas should chase money; money should never chase ideas.

Financial Risk Should Complement the Business Risk

Business risk is the expected volatility of cash flows that is inherent to the nature of a business or its industry. For instance, some businesses will have a demand for their products or services regardless of how the economy is doing. Other types of businesses are dependent on the economy or dependent on trends or fads for success. Likewise, some businesses are very cyclical in their nature. These types of businesses are all considered to have high business risk.

Financial risk is when the financing is structured so that it creates a greater impact on the business's outcome than business risk alone. Consider Figure 2.1, which illustrates the point.

Figure 2.1 illustrates the financial outcomes for two businesses that are identical with the exception of how they are financed. Both companies are financed with $1,000, but Low Fin Risk company has all equity financing and no debt financing, while High Fin Risk company has $800 of debt and only $200 of equity in its capital structure. Figure 2.1 shows three potential scenarios for each of the companies: a Low Sales Case, an Expected Sales Case, and a High Sales Case. It is assumed that the interest cost on the debt is 10 percent.

	Low Fin Risk			High Fin Risk		
Sales	Low	Average	High	Low	Average	High
Gross Profits	50	100	150	50	100	150
Interest Charge	0	0	0	80	80	80
Net Profits	50	100	150	-30	20	70
Equity	1000	1000	1000	200	200	200
Debt	0	0	0	800	800	800
Return on Equity	5%	10%	15%	-15%	10%	35%

Figure 2.1   Illustration of financial risk

From Figure 2.1, we see that the gross profit of the Low Fin Risk company is always positive for our three assumed levels of sales, while the High Fin Risk company will actually have a loss under the Low Sales assumption. More significantly, when the Return on Equity (Net Profits divided by the Equity invested) is calculated we can see that the range of the Return on Equity for the Low Fin Risk company is from 5 percent to 15 percent. The range for the Return on Equity is much larger though for the High Fin Risk company, extending from a negative 5 percent to a positive 35 percent.

This admittedly highly stylized example illustrates the general principle that increasing levels of debt increases the range of returns. Higher amounts of financial risk will mean that outcomes are better in good economic scenarios and conversely outcomes will be worse in bad economic scenarios. The increase in debt, or financial risk, magnifies the economic outcomes.

Again, it is important to remember that the definition of risk is that bad or good things may happen; risk is not simply that only bad things may happen. We see this in the example shown in Figure 2.1. When sales are high, the High Fin Risk company does significantly better than the Low Fin Risk company. This is an example of "good" risk. Conversely when sales are low, the High Fin Risk company does significantly worse, an example of "bad" risk.

To account for this effect, it is a general rule that high–business risk companies should, all else being equal, have lower levels of financial risk. Likewise, low–business risk companies should, all else being equal, have higher levels of financial risk.

The Goal of the Small Business Manager Is to Maximize Utility, Not Wealth

The goal of everybody, and particularly the small business manager, is to remember that the ultimate objective is to maximize utility (happiness and quality of life), which is not necessarily the same as maximizing wealth.

In Chapter 1 we stressed that small business operators often have many objectives beyond the purely financial. These nonfinancial benefits (and admittedly headaches) of managing a small business are what makes it so rewarding. This last principle in this chapter is to remind the small business manager that their objective is to keep their focus on the bigger picture of why they decided to become a small business operator in the first place.

Publicly traded corporations have as part of their legal mandate to maximize shareholder wealth, which is equivalent to maximizing the stock price of the company. This focus on wealth maximization leads to many of the criticisms of capitalism and its short-term focus on share price.[3] Small business owners are not limited by this legal criterion, nor should they be.

Economists assume that rational people want to maximize wealth, solely because wealth is easier to measure than utility. Additionally, everyone has a different utility, a different set of criteria that makes them happy. While wealth is much easier for an economist to develop theoretical models with, it should not imply that it is a good yardstick for the small business operator to use.

---

[3]We remind readers that the exception to this focus on shareholder wealth is the special form of incorporation called a Benefit Corporation. See footnote 4 in Chapter 1.

When making business decisions, and when making financial decisions, the small business manager needs to take into account all of the objectives that led them to work in a small business in the first place. Issues such as freedom, flexibility to be one's own boss, or to follow one's passion should trump maximizing wealth (although the assumed priority of many business owners is maximizing wealth). While wealth is important, and indeed wealth must be created in order for the business to be sustainable, it is not the only criteria.

Concluding Thoughts

Best business and financial management practices have developed over a long period of time. In this chapter we have attempted to bring forward some of the most important general financial management principles that we and others have observed as best practices for small business. Small business management is not a science, and we do not want to suggest that the principles put forward in this chapter are hard and fast rules—they are not. However, these general principles are important and useful to keep in mind. We will be referring to them frequently throughout this book.

CHAPTER 3

Financial Statements

This chapter and the next discuss the main financial statements and their interpretation. Understanding the financial statements is an important part of running a small business. The financial statements are a key record of how the business is doing and provide clues as to what changes might improve the business. Furthermore, the financial statements are a key communication link to the various stakeholders of the business, and none more important than the financial backers of the business.

Despite their importance and central position in running a business, the understanding and interpretation of the financial statements is not always straightforward. In this chapter we introduce the key components of the financial statements and the basic elements that the small business manager needs to be aware of to effectively utilize the various types of financial statements. Special emphasis is placed on interpreting a set of managerially based financial statements that aid in the management of the business as opposed to developing financial statements solely for regulatory or tax purposes. The goal is to make you an effective business manager and not an accountant.

The emphasis in this chapter will be on understanding the key components of the financial statements. The following chapter will focus on analyzing the financial statements in order to make better financial and business decisions.

To aid in the understanding of the financial statements, and to provide examples, we will use the statements that are presented in Figures 3.1 and 3.2. They show the financial statements for Lake Ridge Winery. The following vignette introduces the basic history and context of Lake Ridge Winery.

Lake Ridge Winery

Lake Ridge Winery, a small winery and microbrewery, was on the verge of expanding their operations in a small town that was located just less than 90 minutes from a city with a population of just over 300,000. The proprietors, a husband and wife team, had started the winery as a part-time hobby. Almost by accident it grew into a small business as they got a license and started to sell their product through local county markets that operated on weekends. Further expansions along the way led to the development of a "pop-up" restaurant that operated on their farm on select Saturday nights during tourist season. This "hobby" business had surprisingly early success, but the couple remained in their professional jobs and outsourced most of the day-to-day activities of the company.

As their personal financial situation improved, they started to scale back their "day jobs" and focused on developing the winery and a supporting restaurant into a full-time business that would support them. In fact, the wife had left her full-time job 3 years ago to focus on the business development of the winery. Now it was time for the both of them to devote their collective efforts full time to the business. Family and friends provided most of the financing that they would need to get started, but they also had an investment from a local "angel investor" who believed in the couple's dream and who also wanted to encourage local entrepreneurship.

They had spent almost 3 months planning the expansion of the restaurant portion of the business and years to get the grapes for the wines just right. In order to ensure a quality product, they engaged the services of a wine consultant who had previously produced a wine that received a perfect score of 100 points from a well-known regional wine magazine. Over the past 4 years, the consultant was able to help them perfect their Cabernet Sauvignon grapes and achieve the right brix count for their wine. As the grand opening was approaching the owners knew what they had in the bank, but they had no real plan on how they would track their financials, although this was a requirement for both the bank and their outside investors.

The husband and wife team had an accountant develop their financial statements for the last 3 years (as shown in Figures 3.1 and 3.2),

20X1-20X3 Income Statement - Lake Ridge Winery			
Revenue	20X1	20X2	20X3
Wine Sales	562,847	985,231	1,338,778
Beer	128,031	156,257	205,965
Food Sales	246,815	375,483	473,721
Merchandise	76,285	270,569	308,948
Total Revenue	1,013,978	1,787,540	2,327,412
Cost of sales			
Wages and benefits	77,328	125,724	163,695
Purchases	422,998	659,325	818,473
Total COGS	500,326	785,049	982,168
Gross Profit	513,652	1,002,491	1,345,244
Operating expenses			
Labour and commissions	187,258	282,969	426,981
Depreciation	91,460	175,504	156,457
Repairs and maintenance	8,595	31,258	47,852
Utilities and telecommunication	18,327	22,541	32,586
Interest and bank charges	128,771	128,683	138,228
Professional and business fees	28,996	46,878	44,221
Advertising and promotion	121,328	106,325	95,214
Delivery & shipping expenses	8,578	18,684	28,789
Insurance	12,657	14,987	18,358
Management fees	-	100,000	200,000
Total Operating Expenses	605,969	927,829	1,188,686
Income Before Tax	- 92,317	74,662	156,559
Income Taxes		6,600	13,840
Net Income	- 92,317	68,062	142,719

Figure 3.1 Lake Ridge Winery Income Statement

but understanding their financial situation was anything but straightforward. For instance, questions such as how the expansion would affect their profits, whether they would have the financial resources to sustain the expansion of the business, whether they would be able to attract new financing, and what would happen financially if sales growth slowed due to an economic contraction.

As this business case illustrates there is lots to think about when operating a small business. One of the key factors is to have a solid understanding of the financials of the business. Furthermore, it does not matter

20X1-20X3 Balance Sheet Lake Ridge Winery			
	20X1	20X2	20X3
Assets			
Current Assets			
Cash	$99,399	$143,019	$365,138
Accounts Receivable	7,259	17,887	36,556
Inventory	11,834	33,693	42,394
Total Current Assets	118,492	194,599	444,088
Fixed Assets			
Land	540,000	540,000	540,000
Building	2,093,226	2,093,226	2,093,226
Equipment	600,615	656,000	656,000
Accumulated Depreciation	(91,460)	(266,964)	(423,421)
Total Net Fixed Assets	3,142,381	3,022,262	2,865,805
Total Assets	3,260,873	3,216,861	3,309,893
Liabilities & Equity			
Current Liabilities			
Accounts Payable	88,358	56,497	95,361
Accrued Liabilities	3,195	5,832	8,129
Total Current Liabilities	91,553	62,329	103,490
Long Term Liabilities			
Bank Loan	1,723,534	1,647,630	1,573,241
Other Long Term Liabilities	32,014	24,628	14,699
Total Long Term Liabilities	1,755,548	1,672,258	1,587,940
Total Liabilities	1,847,101	1,734,587	1,691,430
Equity			
Capital Stock	1,500,000	1,500,000	1,500,000
Retained Earnings		(92,317)	(24,255)
Current Year Earnings	(92,317)	68,062	142,719
Total Equity	1,407,683	1,475,745	1,618,463
Total Liabilities & Equity	3,254,784	3,210,332	3,309,893

Figure 3.2 Lake Ridge Winery Balance Sheet

whether your business is thriving or struggling; it is equally important to understand how your business is doing financially. Finally, it makes no difference if your business is growing or maturing; there still needs to be fundamental understanding of your financial statements.

Introduction to the Financial Statements

Being able to interpret and analyze the financial statements of a small business is an essential skill in order to understand how a business is doing financially. The financial statements are the main source of information that we use for financial management of the business. Unfortunately, the financial statements must satisfy the financial information demands of a variety of different stakeholders. It is not only the business owners and managers who need to use the financial statements. Bankers, current and potential investors, suppliers, tax authorities, regulators as well as a variety of other stakeholders will depend on the information in the financial statements to make judgments about the business. This plethora of interested financial stakeholders means that the statements need to be constructed so as to be as useful as possible to as many different users as possible. While this aids in disseminating financial information about the business, it also means that there are elements in the creation of the financial statements that may distort or be confusing to the different users.

Financial statements are created using what is known as Generally Accepted Accounting Principles, which is more commonly known as GAAP accounting or even more simply as just GAAP. These accounting principles create a standard set of accounting rules that allow for consistent understanding of accounting statements across all companies, even though the businesses may be from very different industries. The consistency of GAAP also makes it easier for users of financial statements to understand them.[1]

The primary users of financial statements are the bankers and the financial investors in a business. Bankers are interested in the flow of cash, the stability of the cash flow, and the ratio of the cash flow to the necessary expenses of the firm, including any interest or contractual payments that the business needs to make. Investors are also interested in these variables, but they are also interested in the growth of the cash flows, as equity investors are interested in the growth of their investment, rather than simply ensuring that they will be paid back. This difference between the interests of banks (or debt investors) and equity investors is a key distinction for the business manager looking for financing to keep in mind. Other equity holders may be more concerned about the financial stability as they are dependent on dividends from the business. This is often the

---

[1]U.S. GAAP is widely used in the preparation of financial statements for small businesses. There is also an alternative—the International Financial Reporting Standards or IFRS, for short, which also follow GAAP. The simplified IFRS for small and medium enterprises (SMEs) may be an option compared with the more sophisticated U.S. GAAP.

case for family-owned business, where several family members may be dependent on a steady stream of dividend payments in order to maintain their lifestyle.

Short-term creditors, such as suppliers who have forwarded supplies and goods to the business on credit terms, are interested in the short-term prospects of the business and their current level of liquidity. Potential customers may also request the financial statements for similar reasons as they do not want to submit a large order only to have the business go defunct before they can deliver on the order.

The IRS is obviously concerned that the financial statements accurately reflect the sales and expenses of the business as they pertain to the calculation of taxes that are owed. Regulators meanwhile are concerned that the statements are following GAAP (or other allowed accounting principles) so there is an assurance that the various stakeholders are getting an accurate and consistent picture of the financial health of the business.

The interesting thing is that each group has a different need and a different type of information requirement from the statements. GAAP accounting principles create a consistent set of guidelines that users have confidence will be applied in the construction of any set of financial statements that apply GAAP. Since different users have different needs, they will adjust GAAP accordingly to meet their individual needs.

Of course, the most important users of the financial statements are the business's managers, who need to make decisions about investments and strategies to maintain and grow the business most efficiently. The managers need to use the financial statements for a variety of tasks, and it is quite common for a business to effectively keep up to three sets of financial statements. They will have GAAP statements for reporting purposes, a differently constructed set of financial statements that reflect the realities of the tax code, and a third set of statements called "managerial statements" that are modified to make business decision-making easier.

Before actually discussing the components of the financial statements, it is important to discuss two factors that need to be kept in mind when using the financial statements for business decision making. The first is that the financial statements are historical in nature—they are looking at what happened in the past. However, financial decisions need to be made in regard to anticipated future results, which may or may not be a continuation of the trend from past results. The second aspect is that accounting statements are based on accrual rather than cash accounting. Financial decisions should in theory and in practice be based on cash and cash flows.

One of the confusing aspects of GAAP accounting is that it is accrual, rather than cash based. For example, consider when a sale is made on credit. When a sale is made on credit, the customer may have 90 days to pay the invoice. In accounting terms this gives rise to a Sale, as well as an Accounts Receivable. However, no cash is received at the time of the sale. There is a mismatch in the reporting of the sale and the receipt of the cash flows.

A second accrual accounting example is that of the Depreciation account. Take, for instance, a manufacturing company that has extensive manufacturing equipment. The equipment will obviously wear out and need to be replaced. To account for the forthcoming expense, which may not be for several years, the accountants record a yearly Depreciation charge. Conceptually the Depreciation charge is to account for an accumulating expense that will reflect the fact that the manufacturing equipment will eventually need to be replaced. The tax authorities will also allow for a depreciation expense (called the Modified Accelerated Cost Recovery System or MACRS) to be applied when calculating the company's taxes for the period. However, although the Depreciation is treated as an expense, there is no actual cash flow (assuming that the equipment being depreciated has not yet been replaced). To further confuse the issue, the Depreciation as calculated by GAAP is generally not the same as the MACRS allowed for tax purposes. Meanwhile for the business manager who is concerned with the cash balance available to make payments such as payroll, the accounting statements show an expense for the period that does not apply to the bank balance.

These two accrual examples (and there are many more) show why accounting can be so confusing for the noninitiated. Accrual accounting is very successful in understanding the long-term financial health of a business but can lead to distortions when calculating both short-term and long-term cash flows. Additionally, accrual accounting can lead to distortions in the valuation of the business. This is unfortunate as it is ultimately the cash flows and the valuation that are generally the major concerns for the business manager.

In the sections that follow we will focus on the financial statements from the point of view of the business manager. We suggest you consult a professional accountant for other uses.

There are three main components of the financial statement: the Income Statement, the Balance Sheet, and the Statement of Cash Flows. They each give a piece of the puzzle of how the business is doing.

Income Statement

As its name suggests, the Income Statement shows the income generated by the business in a given time period. It shows the sales of the business as well as the expenses incurred to produce those sales.

Looking at Figure 3.1 Revenues of Lake Ridge Winery have been separated into their major product lines of wine sales, beer sales, food sales, and other merchandise. The breakdown of sales is very helpful for the managers to see how the mix of their business is changing over time.

The expenses incurred in making those sales are broken down into two main components: Cost of Sales and Operating Expenses. Cost of Sales is also frequently called Cost of Goods Sold. It is the cost of the raw materials that produced the items for sale. It includes any inventory or raw materials purchased as well as charges for the labor that went into making the sale items. Operating Expenses are the expenses that are not directly related to any given sale. This includes expenses such as rent, utilities, and interest charges.

The Cost of Sales is closely related to what is known as Variable Costs. These are costs that will vary as the sales vary. If sales increase, then variable costs will also correspondingly increase. There is generally little that the managers can do to affect Cost of Sales for a given sales volume. For instance, if Lake Ridge wants to sell more bottles of wine, they will need to produce more grapes and buy more bottles and incur the expenses for both. They may be able to find cheaper suppliers or change the mix or quality of products that they sell, but that is about it. The greater the amount of sales, the higher the Cost of Sales will be.

Operating Expenses are related to Fixed Costs. As the name suggests, Fixed Costs remain relatively independent of how much is actually sold in the period. They are costs that the business will incur whether they sell a little or they sell a lot. Business managers have a little bit more control over some of their Operating Expenses.

The Revenue minus the Cost of Sales gives what is known as the Gross Profit. It is reflective of the markup or Gross Profit Margin on Sales. The Revenue minus all expenses, including Cost of Sales, as well as Operating Expenses and even Taxes, gives the Net Income for the period. Managers of the business can use the Net Income to pay dividends to shareholders, and what is left over after paying dividends gets reinvested into the business as Retained Earnings. Lake Ridge decided to not pay a dividend and thus they reinvested all of the Net Income back into the business. This Addition to Retained Earnings, which some companies choose to show on their Income Statement, is reflected on the Balance Sheet as Current Year Earnings, where it gets added to the cumulative account Retained Earnings, which is part of Equity. The Addition to Retained Earnings is the link between the Income Statement and the Balance Sheet.

It is important to remember that the Net Income, also known as the Net Profit, is not necessarily the net cash generated by the business for the period due to the effect of accrual accounting.

So what is considered a good Net Income? Well that depends. Is the business growing or stagnant? Is this a new or an existing business? What is the aim of the business—is it to maximize profits or is to minimize taxes paid through tax planning? As you can see from this response the answer to the question of what is considered a good Net Income is "it depends." However, one thing is for sure you do not want to have a negative Net Income for extended periods of time. As Warren Buffet says, "Rule number one of investing is never lose money and rule number two is never forget rule number one!" While Net Income is not directly related to cash flow, over an extended period of time, the two measures should become more closely related.

One key aspect to note about Lake Ridge's Income Statement is that their Net Income is positive, and furthermore is growing over time. As previously stated, financial statements are static, that is, they are "pictures" of the financial performance of a business for a specific period of time. Therefore, it is not necessarily what the statements say about the financial well-being of a business for one period that is important, but instead what the trend is showing is generally of greater importance. Lake

Ridge's Net Income trend is strongly positive, which is a strong indicator of good financial health and a strong business. The issue for Lake Ridge is that as they expand and change their business model, the financial health of the firm may change dramatically. Therefore, a careful consideration of the differences in the financial statements after the period of expansion is warranted to see what the differences are and what has changed.

The Balance Sheet

The Balance Sheet, sometimes called the Statement of Financial Position, tells us what assets and liabilities a company has. The difference between assets and liabilities is called Shareholder's Equity or Net Worth. Like the Income Statement it measures activities from the past. It also is based on accrual accounting. These two factors mean that Shareholder's Equity, as stated on the Balance Sheet, can be significantly distorted from the true equity value of the firm. We will discuss this point in more depth later in this section.

The Balance Sheet is separated into two main sections: Assets, and then Liabilities and Equity. In turn, Assets is divided into Current Assets and Fixed Assets. Likewise, Liabilities and Equity is separated into three sections: Current Liabilities, Long-Term Liabilities, and Equity.

As the name suggests, assets are the positive value items contained in the business. Current or Short-Term Assets are those items that, conceptually at least, could be turned into cash within a year. They include the following: Cash, which is self-explanatory; Accounts Receivable, which are amounts owed to the firm by its customers; and Inventory, which are raw materials or finished goods that are ready for sale. Fixed Assets include longer lasting or more permanent items such as the building and equipment that the firm owns.

Short-Term Liabilities are the obligations that, conceptually at least, need to be paid for within the year. These include the following: Accounts Payable, which are amounts owed to vendors and suppliers to the firm; Accrued Liabilities, which may include items such as unpaid wages to workers or other fees and dues. Also, any short obligations coming due within a year would be included in Current Liabilities, such as any short-term bank loans. Long-Term Liabilities are the major long-lasting obligations of the business, such as any bank loans or mortgages.

Finally, there is the Equity portion of the Balance Sheet. This section includes the Capital Stock, which is the value of equity, including any initial equity that the owners of the firm put directly into the business. The Retained Earnings are the accumulated portion of the Net Income that has been reinvested into the business throughout the history of the business.

The Balance Sheet gets its name from the fact that the total amount of the Assets must equal the total amount of the sum of the Liabilities as well as the Equity of the firm. The Assets are what the firm owns, and from a possession viewpoint, they represent what the firm is worth. The Liabilities combined with the Equity is how those assets have been financed. Subtracting the Liabilities from the Assets gives the net value of the firm. This subtraction also gives the value of the Total Equity. Thus, conceptually at least, the Total Equity is the value of the company from the owner's point of view. This accounting measure of the value of the firm is generally highly distorted for the reasons mentioned earlier, namely, the accrual nature of accounting, as well as the fact that the value of the firm should be based on its forward-looking prospects. In addition, it is difficult for standard accounting to take into account valuable aspects of a business, such as its customer loyalty, any proprietary processes it may have, or the business intelligence and competitiveness of its managers. For this reason, the Equity as measured by the accountants generally understates the true value of the business. In certain situations, this understatement of value may be significant. This effect is easily observed by looking at the value of publicly traded corporations and the accounting value based on the Total Equity shown on their Balance Sheets.[2]

As with the Income Statement, it is key to look at the Balance Sheet over a period of time. As might be expected, given the strong performance trend exhibited by the Income Statement, the Total Equity shows a strong upward trend, which is a key positive indicator. The following chapter will go into much more detail on analyzing and interpreting both the Income Statement and the Balance Sheet.

---

[2]As an example, at the time of this writing in early February 2020, the accounting value in the equity section for the car maker Tesla was $7.5 billion, while the market value of the equity, as calculated on the basis of its traded stock price, was $140.5 billion.

The Cash Flow Statement

A third financial statement, called the Cash Flow Statement, is also generally constructed for a firm. The Cash Flow Statement, or Statement of Cash Flows as it is also referred to as, shows the cash generated and used during a specific period of time. The Cash Flow Statement complements the Income Statement. It links the Income Statement to the changes in the Balance Sheet from one year to the next. It shows how the changes in the Income Statement and Balance Sheet come about through the changes in cash, and more importantly, how those changes in cash have been generated. The Cash Flow Statement breaks the cash flows of the business into three separate activities of the firm: Operating Activities, Investing Activities, and Financing Activities.

The Cash Flow Statement helps the business manager see where cash flows are being generated and where they are being used. In other words, where a company gets its money (cash inflows) and where it spends its money (cash outflows).

The Cash Flow Statement is important for three main reasons. First, it indicates how liquid a company is over time rather than a specific amount at a given point in time. Second, it is also a useful tool to decipher whether or not a company is viable in the short term. However, most importantly, the Statement of Cash Flows shows whether the business is generating positive cash flows from Operating Activities versus generating Cash Flows solely from Financing or Investing Activities. The Income Statement only shows profitability, but it does not clearly show cash flows and where exactly the cash flows come from. That is the job of the Statement of Cash Flows. However, the Cash Flow Statement does not show profitability. You need to look at the Income Statement for this.

The Cash Flow Statement for Lake Ridge Winery is shown in Figure 3.3.

The Operating Activities are the portion of the Cash Flow Statement that shows how much cash is made from the sales of services and products. The cash generated here is the key source of cash! Therefore, if there is strong cash flow from operations there is a good chance the company is in good financial shape. This is especially true if there is a trend of strong

20X1-20X3
Cash Flow - Lake Ridge Winery

	20X1	20X2	20X3
Operating activities			
Net income	$ (92,317)	$68,062	$142,719
Items not requiring an outlay of funds			
Depreciation	91,460	175,504	156,457
Changes in non-cash working capital			
Accounts receivables	(7,259)	(10,628)	(18,669)
Prepaid expenses & deposits		-	
Inventory	(11,834)	(21,859)	(8,701)
Accounts payable	88,358	(31,861)	38,864
Accrued Liabilities	3,195	2,637	2,297
	71,602	**181,855**	**312,967**
Investing activities			
Acquisition of property, plant and equipment	(3,233,841)	(55,385)	-
Loans to (from) related companies			
Loans to (from) shareholders	-	-	
	(3,233,841)	**(55,385)**	**-**
Financing activities			
Proceeds from issuance of shares	1,500,000		
Proceeds from (repayment of) loans	1,761,638	(82,850)	(90,848)
	3,261,638	**(82,850)**	**(90,848)**
Increase (decrease) in cash and cash equivalents	**99,399**	**43,620**	**222,119**
Cash and cash equivalents, beginning of year	-	99,399	143,019
Cash and cash equivalents, end of year	**$99,399**	**$143,019**	**$365,138**

Figure 3.3 Lake Ridge Winery Cash Flow Statement

cash flow in this area. For Lake Ridge we see that Cash from Operating Activities is positive for both years.

A significant part of the Cash from Operating Activities to note is Changes in Noncash Working Capital. This section creates part of the conversion from accrual accounting to cash-based accounting, and is also a large part of the reason why it is called the Cash Flow Statement. On the Balance Sheet for Lake Ridge (Figure 3.2), you will note that Accounts

Receivable went from 7,259 to 17,887 from year 20X1 to 20X2. This is an increase of 10,628. This increase in Accounts Receivable represents an increase in Sales that the customers have not yet paid for. In other words, it is Sales that the accountants have recorded that have not yet been received as cash. This amount is thus subtracted on the Cash Flow Statement to reflect this reality. Similar adjustments are made for cash changes between accrual accounting and cash flows for Depreciation, Inventory, and Accounts Payable. For instance, Depreciation of 91,460 is added back to Cash From Operating Activities as the accounting statements subtracted this amount for Depreciation even though no such cash outflow occurred. The adding back of the 91,460 reflects this. Through such adjustments, the cash flows of the business can be more clearly seen by using the Statement of Cash Flows.

Under the Cash from Investing Activities section any changes in equipment, assets, or investments are recorded and the associated cash flow impact. Most of these transactions are a use of cash (cash outflows) as they are used to purchase equipment, investments, and assets. To stay current and invest in the future, many healthy companies spend money in this category on a regular basis, as we see that Lake Ridge has done.

The Cash from Financing Activities relates to changes in various loans, equity infusions, and other sources of capital. When a company borrows or raises capital it is considered a cash inflow versus when dividends are paid, debt is paid down, or capital is repaid; then it is a cash outflow. One of the key distortions that the Statement of Cash Flows illustrates and that the Income Statement can disguise is the overuse of Financing Activities to hide an unstainable amount of negative cash flows from Operating Activities. Aside from their initial large start-up cash infusion, we see that Lake Ridge was able to sustain their business in the second year of operations without an additional infusion of cash and instead was able to rely on their cash flow from operations to continue to invest in maintaining and growing the business. This is a good sign.

Using the Financial Statements

Now that the basic items in the financial statements are understood, it is important to use them. The following chapter goes over an analysis of the financial statements, but a few comments are in order before we get to the specifics of analysis.

The first thing is that the financial statements should be used as a valuable tool or set of measures for managing the business. The financial statements should not simply be seen as a regulatory necessity or as a requirement solely for the financial stakeholders in the business. The financial statements should be examined each period that they are constructed. They tell a story about the evolution of the business and how well it is doing, or the challenges it is having. The financial statements provide important clues as to the important drivers of the business and provide suggestions for managerial action.

The profit and loss of a business are crucial for the survival of the business. It is therefore important that you understand what is included, what each component is, and what it means to the business. Get familiar with what drives each component. For example, for a business like a winery, it is important to understand what drives cost of goods sold. There are inputs such as grapes, bottles, and labelling, but another important aspect is labor. The labor cost involved in picking the grapes and the actual production costs to produce the final product (corks, bottles, labels, grapes, supplies) are crucial to understand gross profit and overall profitability of the business.

Financial statements can quickly become complex and hard to understand so it is important that they are created with the end user in mind. As a business owner you should get involved as these are being created and see if they make sense—are there too many categories or not enough detail? Getting that balance will be key for your success. As the operator of the business if you don't have a good grasp of what is happening and how you make money, then you must make the time to understand. This investment will pay benefits in the future as the company grows but also during challenging periods. You will be able to course correct through the diagnosis of what is happening and get back on track.

There are many ways to learn about financial statements and there is no right or wrong way as long as you get comfortable with them. Each company's financial statements will have unique components, so it is not possible to have a generic set of accounting descriptions that will apply in all situations. You may know someone who is a mentor that can show you how the financials work, or it may be an expert in the field that you hire. As long as you get a good understanding of the key areas, you will be in good shape. Hopefully this chapter gives you a solid introductory understanding.

Depending on the business it may be that labor costs are more important (think labor intensive businesses like a call center) or food costs (as in a restaurant), but in either case a business must understand these main cost drivers in order to understand and manage the business. With experience these may become second nature, but in the early days and even when a business is growing or struggling, knowing the key components is very important for the long-term success. The same holds true for the revenue. What are the key things that the business makes money on? What are the areas of the business that produce the best margins? What items is the business actually losing money on? What areas of the business produce the best net positive cash flows? These are all questions that the accounting statements can help answer.

Some Concluding Thoughts

In this chapter we have covered each of the components of financial statements, what they mean, and their uses. We have also discussed the challenges of using historical information from the financial statements and the accounting versus finance view of the company financials. The key points to take away from this chapter are what the various components are and what they mean. Ultimately, how financial statements are crafted, and how they are interpreted, really depends on the business—they need to be specific for that business. However, what is common for all businesses is to strive to have quality information to feed the financial statements. Otherwise the business faces the adage "Garbage in equals garbage out," and the financials will not be useful to run the business.

For businesses it is essential to look at its cash flow on a frequent basis and not just rely on the Income Statement to determine financial health. Do not forget the Balance Sheet either. The Balance Sheet is important because it shows what the business is owed (Accounts Receivable) and what the company needs to pay out for bills (Accounts Payable and Accrued Liabilities). It provides the information that stakeholders will use to make decisions about the company. Each stakeholder will have a different set of analysis and metrics that they will use, which is the subject of the next chapter.

It is important for the business manager to understand their financial statements as it is the financial statements that are the main communication tool to external financial stakeholders of the business. Banks and investors will use the financial statements to make judgments about the firm. The manager that can best use the financial statements to tell the story of how their business is successful and will continue to be successful is the business manager that will have a competitive advantage in securing financing at reasonable rates.

Something to keep in mind is that it is better to review the financials on a more frequent basis than not. This will allow identification of any challenges with the business in order to course correct. Likewise if the business is doing well it may be a good time to expand the business or set aside money that can be used as a cushion to sop up losses when things are not going so well or for a business where seasonality is a factor.

Financial Statements are not just a recording of the transactions of a business; they are also a tool to use to evaluate the business and for decision making. Throughout the rest of this book we will refer to various sections or items of the financial statements. The next chapter will focus on financial statement analysis.

CHAPTER 4

Financial Metrics

In the previous chapter we introduced the main components of the financial statements. This chapter focuses on analyzing those financial statements as well as a few other important parameters that are used for successful financial management. This chapter reviews the basics of data analysis as well as ratio analysis. It will form the basis of the following chapter, which looks at planning and forecasting.

Having data is great, but data alone cannot tell you much. What is necessary is an analysis and interpretation of the data. One of the key principles for managing data is to realize that a business is not a static activity and thus looking at the data on a static basis in not that helpful or insightful. What is much more important is the trend of the data, and if applicable (or available), what is the trend relative to a peer group or industry expectations.

Another key principle of data analysis is to realize that different stakeholders will take a different view of the different financial metrics of the firm. For a common example, equity stakeholders will applaud significant sales growth while creditors of the firm, including suppliers, may see aggressive sales growth as a cause for concern that the firm is growing faster than its capability to both manage that growth and finance the growth.

A final point to remember is that financial analysis is as much of an art as it is a science. Factors beyond the control of the company may change, new fads or trends may develop, and unintended consequences of management actions are always a possibility. If finance and management was a science, then all businesses would be run by a bot and there would not be a need for managers in the first place. Data analysis helps in decision making, but ultimately the intuition, humility, and managerial flexibility of the manager will trump cold, hard, analytical data analysis.

We begin by looking at some ways to examine the trend analysis. Throughout this chapter we will use the financial statements of Lake Ridge Winery that were given in Figures 3.1 to 3.3 of the previous chapter.

Trend Analysis

As stated, the trend in finance is often more important and insightful than the actual level of a variable or a ratio. Finance is both dynamic and forward looking, so the purpose of most of the analysis is to try to ascertain what the future is going to hold in order to best plan for it. Unfortunately, or perhaps fortunately, trends in finance are rarely a linear progression. An old finance adage states, "Just when you think it is a trend, you find out it is a cycle." However, trends can give us clues about what happened and what might happen.

A common technique to aid in the spotting of trends in the financial statements is to convert the financial statements into what is known as "common size" statements. To do this, each of the figures of the Income Statement are calculated as a percentage of Sales, and all of the figures of the Balance Sheet are shown as a percentage of Total Assets. The Common Size Income Statement is shown in Figure 4.1, and the Common Size Balance Sheet is shown in Figure 4.2.

From the Common Size Income Statement, we can see that the growth in gross profit from 51 to 58 percent has come about mainly through the reduction of the purchases from 42 percent of total revenues to just 35 percent of total revenues. We also see that other expenses have stayed relatively constant with the exception of bank charges and advertising, both of which have fallen significantly. However, management fees have risen significantly, presumably as a consequence of the increasing profits making the managers more comfortable paying themselves a larger salary. Overall, the increase in Gross Profit, and decreases in bank charges as well as advertising expenses, has led to the company going from a loss position to a profit position, despite the significant increase in management fees. This is the power of a Common Size Income Statement as it makes these trends in revenues, expenses, and profits very easy to spot and identify.

The Common Size Balance Sheet also makes trends easy to spot, although for Lake Ridge there were not any significantly outstanding trend changes as their Balance Sheet relationships have stayed relatively stable.

20X1-20X3 Common Size Income Statement - Lake Ridge Winery			
Revenue	20X1	20X2	20X3
Wine Sales	0.56	0.55	0.58
Beer	0.13	0.09	0.09
Food Sales	0.24	0.21	0.20
Merchandise	0.08	0.15	0.13
Total Revenue	1.00	1.00	1.00
Cost of sales			
Wages and benefits	0.08	0.07	0.07
Purchases	0.42	0.37	0.35
Total COGS	0.49	0.44	0.42
Gross Profit	0.51	0.56	0.58
Operating expenses			
Labour and commissions	0.18	0.16	0.18
Depreciation	0.09	0.10	0.07
Repairs and maintenance	0.01	0.02	0.02
Utilities and telecommunication	0.02	0.01	0.01
Interest and bank charges	0.13	0.07	0.06
Professional and business fees	0.03	0.03	0.02
Advertising and promotion	0.12	0.06	0.04
Delivery & shipping expenses	0.01	0.01	0.01
Insurance	0.01	0.01	0.01
Management fees	-	0.06	0.09
Total Operating Expenses	0.60	0.52	0.51
Income Before Tax	0.09	0.04	0.07
Income Taxes	-	0.00	0.01
Net Income	0.09	0.04	0.06

Figure 4.1 Common size income statement

In the following sections we will examine a large number of financial ratios. In most cases, tracking these changes through time and understanding the changes through time are more helpful to the manager to look at than the value of a ratio at a given point in time.

Ratio Analysis

It can be very difficult to ascertain whether a given company is doing well simply by looking at the numbers on a financial statement. For instance, if the revenues are $1 million, then that would be excellent for a small

	20X1-20X3 Balance Sheet Lake Ridge Winery		
	20X1	20X2	20X3
Assets			
Current Assets			
Cash	0.03	0.04	0.11
Accounts Receivable	0.00	0.01	0.01
Inventory	0.00	0.01	0.01
Total Current Assets	0.04	0.06	0.13
Fixed Assets			
Land	0.17	0.17	0.16
Building	0.64	0.65	0.63
Equipment	0.18	0.20	0.20
Accumulated Depreciation	(0.03)	(0.08)	(0.13)
Total Net Fixed Assets	0.96	0.94	0.87
Total Assets	1.00	1.00	1.00
Liabilities & Equity			
Current Liabilities			
Accounts Payable	0.03	0.02	0.03
Accrued Liabilities	0.00	0.00	0.00
Total Current Liabilities	0.03	0.02	0.03
Long Term Liabilities			
Bank Loan	0.53	0.51	0.48
Other Long Term Liabilities	0.01	0.01	0.00
Total Long Term Liabilities	0.54	0.52	0.48
Total Liabilities	0.57	0.54	0.51
Equity			
Capital Stock	0.46	0.47	0.45
Retained Earnings	-	(0.03)	(0.01)
Current Year Earnings	(0.03)	0.02	0.04
Total Equity	0.43	0.46	0.49
Total Liabilities & Equity	1.00	1.00	1.00

Figure 4.2 *Common size balance sheet*

single owner-operator proprietorship but an embarrassingly low revenue number for a publicly traded multinational company. However, if it is stated that the company is generating $20 of revenue for every dollar of assets, we can then compare the relative success of the sole proprietorship business with that of the publicly traded multinational.

Ratio analysis not only helps us to compare success across companies, but also success through time. As a business grows and diversifies its product offering, the ratios will also change, and ratio analysis helps the manager to better assess which areas of the business are operating effectively and which might need some management attention.

Ratio analysis is used by a wide number of stakeholders, and especially, by financial stakeholders. Banks use ratio analysis extensively to assess both whether a business will be granted financing and what the terms of the financing will be. Likewise, trade creditors will also use ratio analysis to assess whether to extend credit. Investors are a third important group of stakeholders that rely upon ratio analysis. Thus, it is important that the manager understands how to see their business as others are seeing it. Ratio analysis is not only important to understand as a useful financial management tool, but also as a negotiating tool with external stakeholders.

We will separate the discussion of ratios into four categories that roughly correspond to the management tasks of liquidity, efficiency, financial leverage, and profitability.

Liquidity Ratios

Liquidity refers to the ability of a business to remain solvent, at least in the short term. In essence, liquidity is an indication of the company's ability to pay its day-to-day expenses. The first key ratio to look at is the Days Cash ratio. This is simply the cash on hand divided by the average daily expenses of the firm. For Lake Ridge in 20X3 this is as follows:

$$\text{Days Cash Ratio} = \frac{\text{Available Cash}}{\left(\dfrac{\text{Annual Expenses}}{365}\right)}$$

$$= \frac{365,138}{\left(\dfrac{982,168 + 1,188,686 - 156,457}{365}\right)} = 66.2$$

This Days Cash ratio of 66.2 days basically implies that Lake Ridge could go for 66.2 days without making any sales whatsoever and still be able to meet its expenses payments. Note that the denominator is a combination of the Cost of Sales (982,168) and the Total Operating Expenses (1,188,686) but with the Depreciation subtracted (156,457). The Depreciation is subtracted from the expenses, as the Depreciation is not a cash expense but is included in the Income Statement as a noncash accounting measure.

The Days Cash ratio is critical for start-up firms that are still in the product development stage. For new firms, the Days Cash ratio is an indicator of how long the company has remaining to develop a viable product (or service) and generate sales before they are forced to go out of business or seek additional sources of financing.

The liquidity of the firm is basically the difference between their Current Assets, which are conceptually the assets that could be quickly turned into cash if needed, and the Current Liabilities, which are the liabilities that will be due in the short term. The Current Ratio is thus simply the ratio of the Current Assets to the Current Liabilities. For Lake Ridge Winery for year 20X3, the Current Ratio is as follows:

$$\text{Current Ratio} = \frac{\text{Current Assets}}{\text{Current Liabilities}} = \frac{444{,}088}{103{,}490} = 4.3$$

While it varies by industry, a general rule of thumb is that a Current Ratio of 2 or better is acceptable and provides a comfortable margin for being ability to pay upcoming expenses. However, a very high Current Ratio is a potential sign of inappropriate use of liquid assets. An excessively high Current Ratio is potentially a sign that the business might have too many assets on hand that are not effectively producing profits or cash flows. Such excess assets, for instance, excess cash or excess inventory should be liquidated by investing in profitable activities or returning the cash to investors, who can put the money into other more profitable ventures.

One criticism of the Current Ratio as a measure of short-term liquidity is that it contains inventory as a measure. Inventory, particularly if it is a large portion of the Current Assets, may be old or outdated, and thus the assumption that it could be quickly sold at true value in order to pay liabilities may not be warranted. To counter that reasonable objection, a second liquidity ratio called the Quick Ratio is calculated. The Quick Ratio, also called the Acid Test, is the same as the Current Ratio, only that the value of the inventories is not included in the numerator. The Quick Ratio for Lake Ridge Winery for year 20X3 is as follows:

$$\text{Quick Ratio} = \frac{\text{Current Assets} - \text{Inventory}}{\text{Current Liabilities}} = \frac{444{,}088 - 42{,}394}{103{,}490} = 3.9$$

Another very important number when it comes to liquidity is the earnings before interest and taxes with depreciation and amortization, which is much more commonly called EBITDA. EBITDA is basically an approximation of the cash being generated by the business that can be used to pay all the stakeholders, including creditors (Interest Expenses), the government (Taxes), and of course the equity investors.

To calculate the EBITDA, the Depreciation (and Amortization if any) is first added back to the Income Before Tax. As previously mentioned, Depreciation is not an actual cash flow, but is an accounting measure. Thus, although Depreciation is counted as an expense by the accounting convention, no actual cash flow is associated with it and thus this is excess cash, over the Income Before Tax, that the business has available to it. The Interest is also added back as the objective is to measure the cash generated by business activities before the effect of any financing activities.

EBITDA is not a perfect measure of cash flow, but it provides a reasonable proxy for the actual cash being generated by the business. This is particularly true when the EBITDA is tracked over time.[1] It is thus an important measure of liquidity and indeed of the overall health as well as the value of the business. We will revisit EBITDA when we examine how to value a business.

For 20X3, the EBITDA for Lake Ridge is as follows:

$$EBITDA = \text{Income Before Tax} + \text{Depreciation} + \text{Interest Expense}$$
$$= 156,559 + 156,457 + 138,228 = 451,244$$

Efficiency Ratios

Efficiency ratios examine how efficiently the business is utilizing its assets. Like most ratios, efficiency ratios are very industry dependent, so before determining whether the value that is calculated is too high or too low, one should calibrate one's opinion on the basis of where the calculated ratio is relative to the same ratio of other companies in the same industry.

---

[1] EBITDA is not a perfect measure of cash flow mainly due to the accrual nature of accounting statements. For instance, changes in Accounts Receivable or Accounts Payable from year to year reflect cash flows that have not actually occurred. By tracking EBITDA through time, these accrual accounting effects somewhat tend to even out.

The main efficiency ratio is the Asset Turnover Ratio and there are two versions of it: the Total Asset Turnover Ratio and the Fixed Asset Turnover Ratio. The asset turnover ratios are basically telling how many dollars of sales are generated by a dollar of assets. Obviously the greater the number, the more efficiently the resources of the business are being utilized. The difference between the Total Asset Turnover Ratio and the Fixed Asset Turnover Ratio is, for some industries, an indication of the level of idle infrastructure that the firm has. For Lake Ridge Winery, the Total Asset Turnover and the Fixed Asset Turnover for year 20X3 are, respectively, as follows:

$$\text{Total Asset Turnover} = \frac{\text{Sales}}{\text{Total Assets}} = \frac{2,327,412}{3,309,893} = 0.70$$

$$\text{Fixed Asset Turnover} = \frac{\text{Sales}}{\text{Net Fixed Assets}} = \frac{2,327,412}{2,865,805} = 0.81$$

From these asset turnover ratios we see that Lake Ridge Winery generates 70 cents of revenue for every dollar of Total Assets to generate a dollar of Revenues. When we look at forecasting future cash needs in Chapter 5, this ratio will be key. As a first estimate of the financing needed to grow a business, the Total Asset Turnover gives an estimate of the financing needed to generate additional revenues.

All else being equal, a business would prefer to be able to generate more revenue per dollar of assets, or in other words have a larger Asset Turnover Ratio, and this is particularly so for the Fixed Asset Turnover. A high Fixed Asset Turnover Ratio is generally an indication that the business is running at a high capacity and efficiently utilizing their plant and equipment. However, there is an important caveat about a larger assets turnover ratio always being better. A company with an unusually high Fixed Asset Turnover Ratio value may be an indication that they have not appropriately replaced or upgraded their fixed assets. In these cases, the Fixed Assets Turnover Ratio will increase solely because of the effect of Depreciation on the Net Fixed Assets value. While having a high Fixed Assets Turnover Ratio is desirable, it is not desirable if the high ratio is achieved by neglecting the proper maintenance and modernization of equipment.

Working capital is generally defined as Current Assets minus Current Liabilities. Working capital is the short-term assets of the business, and it is just as important to efficiently manage and utilize the Short-Terms Assets as it is the Long-Term Fixed Assets. There are three important measures for measuring the working capital efficiency: the Days Accounts Receivable, the Days of Inventory, and the Days Accounts Payable.

Days Account Receivable measures how efficient the business is at collecting on invoices from customers. As suggested by the name, it is the average amount of days that it takes the company to collect on its receivables. For Lake Ridge Winery in year 20X3, the Days Accounts Receivable is as follows:

$$\text{Days Accounts Receivable} = 365 \times \frac{\text{Accounts Receivable}}{\text{Revenue}}$$

$$= 365 \times \frac{36,556}{2,327,412} = 5.73$$

Days Accounts Payable measures the amount of time in days that it takes the company to pay its suppliers on average. For Lake Ridge Winery for 20X3, the Days Accounts Payable value is as follows:

$$\text{Days Accounts Payable} = 365 \times \frac{\text{Accounts Payable}}{\text{Total Cost of Goods Sold}}$$

$$= 365 \times \frac{95,361}{982,168} = 35.4$$

In the same spirit of Days Accounts Receivable and Days Accounts Payable, the Days of Inventory Ratio measures the average amount of days that it takes to turn Inventory into sales. For Lake Ridge Winery for 20X3, the Days Inventory value is as follows:

$$\text{Days Inventory} = 365 \times \frac{\text{Inventory}}{\text{Purchases}} = 365 \times \frac{42,394}{818,473} = 18.9$$

In addition to Days Inventory, some companies will also calculate Days Sales Inventory, which presents the number of days that the company can maintain their sales without buying more goods for inventory.

For Lake Ridge Winery for 20X3, the Days Sales Inventory value is as follows:

$$\text{Days Sales Inventory} = 365 \times \frac{\text{Inventory}}{\text{Revenue}} = 365 \times \frac{42,394}{2,327,412} = 6.6$$

Days Accounts Receivable combines with the Days Inventory and Days Accounts Payable to form an important measure of working capital management called the Cash Conversion Cycle, which will be discussed at length in Chapter 7. The Cash Conversion Cycle is a measure of the number of days between when the company has to make payments for raw goods, services, and inventory and the period when the cash comes in from receiving payments from sales. The Cash Conversion Cycle for Lake Ridge Winery for 20X3 is as follows:

$$\text{Cash Conversion Cycle} = \text{Days Accounts Receivable} +$$
$$\text{Days Inventory} - \text{Days Accounts Payble}$$
$$\text{Cash Conversion Cycle} = 5.73 + 18.9 - 35.4 = -10.8$$

Leverage Ratios

Leverage ratios look at the financing mix of the business and the ability of the business to manage its chosen financing mix. The first thing that people think about are the debt ratios, which measure the proportion of the company that is financed with debt. There are a variety of debt ratios and they all tell a slightly different story. The primary debt ratios are the Debt to Total Assets Ratio and the Debt to Equity Ratio. These ratios are looking at the amount of the Long-Term Debt that is financing the long-term capital structure of the firm. For Lake Ridge Winery in 20X3, these two ratios, respectively, are as follows:

$$\text{Debt to Total Assets} = \frac{\text{Total Long} - \text{Term Liabilities}}{\text{Total Assets}} = \frac{1,587,940}{3,309,893} = 0.48$$

$$\text{Debt to Equity} = \frac{\text{Total Long} - \text{Term Liabilities}}{\text{Total Equity}} = \frac{1,587,940}{1,618,463} = 0.98$$

These Long-Term Debt ratios however can be misleading if the company is financing itself with a lot of short-term debt as well. While the general rule is to finance short assets, such as working capital, with short-term debt and equity, and long-term assets, with long-term debt and equity, the practical reality of how companies chose to finance themselves is often quite different.[2] For this reason, it is important to also calculate a Total Debt Ratio, which is given for Lake Ridge Winery for year 20X3 as follows:

$$\text{Total Debt Ratio} = \frac{\text{Total Liabilities}}{\text{Total Assets}} = \frac{1,691,430}{3,309,893} = 0.51$$

Regardless of the amount of debt, the aspect that most creditors are concerned about is the ability of the company to service the debt. This is given by the Interest Coverage Ratio, which is the cash flows coming in divided by the contractual debt payments. The EBITDA is considered to be a proxy for the incoming cash flows available to service the debt, and the Interest Payments as a proxy for the debt obligations. The Interest Coverage Ratio for Lake Ridge Winery for 20X3 is as follows:

$$\text{Interest Coverage Ratio} = \frac{\text{EBITDA}}{\text{Interest}} = \frac{142,719 + 138,228 + 156,457}{138,228} = 3.26$$

The Interest Coverage Ratio might be extended if the company has significant other contractual payments, such as leases, or principal repayments due on their debt. In this case, the Total Coverage Ratio is applicable.

$$\text{Total Coverage Ratio} = \frac{\text{Total Cash Available for Contractual Payments}}{\text{Total Contractual Payments Within Year}}$$

The coverage ratios are generally the key metric that creditors examine when determining whether to lend money to a business. These ratios should be carefully watched and managed.

---

[2] The best practices of choosing a financing strategy are discussed in Chapter 6.

Profitability Ratios

The Net Profit Margin is the Net Income divided by Revenues and measures the overall profitability of the business after all expenses are taken account of. It basically tells what the profits to the equity holders are for each dollar of Revenue. The Net Profit Margin for Lake Ridge Winery for 20X3 is given by the following:

$$\text{Net Profit Margin} = \frac{\text{Net Income}}{\text{Revenue}} = \frac{142,719}{2,327,412} = 0.061 \text{ or } 6.1\%$$

The Gross Profit Margin represents the margin only taking into account the Cost of Goods Sold. For Lake Ridge Winery in 20X3, the Gross Profit Margin is as follows:

$$\text{Gross Profit Margin} = \frac{\text{Revenue} - \text{Cost of Goods Sold}}{\text{Revenue}}$$

$$= \frac{1,345,244}{2,327,412} = 0.58 \text{ or } 58\%$$

The difference between Gross Profit Margin and Net Profit Margin is an indication of how efficient the business is at the necessary, but not income producing, parts of the business. The Net Profit Margin can also be affected by the efficiency of the debt financing.

The next two profitability ratios show the ratio of profit to the amount of capital that has been employed. The Return on Assets measures the profit relative to the total amount of assets used to generate those profits. The Return on Equity measures the profit relative to the amount of equity invested. The difference between the two similar ratios is an indication of the amount of leverage used in the business. A business with a low Return on Assets is a sign of a business that may be being managed inefficiently. Such inefficiency may be masked however with a high Return on Equity, which could be accomplished simply by having an excessively high amount of debt to finance the activities of the firm. The ratios for Lake Ridge Winery for 20X3 are as follows:

$$\text{Return on Assets} = \frac{\text{Net Income}}{\text{Total Assets}} = \frac{142,719}{3,309,893} = 0.04$$

$$\text{Return on Equity} = \frac{\text{Net Income}}{\text{Total Equity}} = \frac{142{,}719}{1{,}618{,}463} = 0.09$$

The Return on Equity is the ratio that the owners of the firm are most interested in. It shows how much profit each dollar of their investment is generating. To further analyze how that profit is being generated, the Return on Equity can be broken into three component parts in what is known as the Dupont Analysis. The Dupont Analysis is a decomposition of the Return on Equity into three components as shown here:

$$\text{Dupont Analysis} = \frac{\text{Net Income}}{\text{Revenue}} \times \frac{\text{Revenue}}{\text{Total Assets}} \times \frac{\text{Total Assets}}{\text{Total Equity}}$$

For Lake Ridge Winery in 20X3, this is as follows:

$$\text{Dupont Analysis} = \frac{142{,}719}{2{,}327{,}412} \times \frac{2{,}327{,}412}{3{,}}309{,}893$$

$$\times \frac{3{,}309{,}893}{1{,}618{,}463} = 0.09 = 9\%$$

Note that the first ratio in the analysis is simply the Net Profit Margin, which is a measure of the ability of the business to generate profits from sales. The second component is the inverse of Total Asset Turnover Ratio, which, as previously discussed, is a measure of the operational or manufacturing efficiency of the business. The third and last component is another measure for leverage in the firm. Thus, the Dupont Analysis decomposes the Return on Equity into a profitability component, an efficiency component, and a leverage component. Tracked through time, changes in the Dupont Analysis components help the equity investors of the business see where their return is being generated and areas of operation where the return might be enhanced.

Examining Ratios through Time

We have mentioned that it is useful to examine how the ratios change through time. The Table shown in Figure 4.3 shows the components of the Dupont Ratio discussed for Lake Ridge Winery and how they have evolved along with the company.

20X1-20X3 Dupont Ratio Analysis - Lake Ridge Winery			
	20X1	20X2	20X3
Net Profit Margin	-0.09	0.04	0.06
Total Asset Turnover	0.31	0.56	0.70
Leverage	2.32	2.18	2.05
Return on Equity	**-0.07**	**0.05**	**0.09**

Figure 4.3   Dupont ratio analysis

From Figure 4.3, we see a clear trend of an increasing Return on Equity being driven by improvements in Net Profit Margin and Total Asset Turnover, while Leverage has decreased slightly. This Dupont Ratio Analysis clearly shows that Lake Ridge Winery is doing an excellent job of improving its margins as well as its operating efficiency. Conversely, if the improvement in the Return on Equity was being driven by a corresponding increase in Leverage, then there would have been much less cause for optimism about the quality of the management at Lake Ridge.

We illustrated the importance of looking at trends through time through the Dupont Ratio Analysis, but we could have just as easily looked at a number of other ratios. In addition to tracking how a company is doing through time, it is also extremely useful to track how a business is doing relative to its industry peers. Various websites publish average ratio values for companies by industry.[3] The industry averages provide a very useful benchmark for a small business to use to judge how they are doing.

One should be careful though to not take industry average comparisons too far. To begin, companies within an industry can have a wide range of operating strategies that will produce a wide range of ratios. Additionally, geographical differences or idiosyncratic factors can mean that a very well-run company may operate with financial ratios very different from the norm.

---

[3]See for example: http://www.bizstats.com/.

Risk Metrics

It was stated at the beginning of this book that finance is about the trade-offs between cash flow and risk, or somewhat equivalently, between return and risk. So far, the ratios that we have discussed deal mainly with the cash flows, returns, and profitability. While there are well-known risk measures for publicly traded corporations, the risk measures for small businesses are fewer in number and more subjective in their application. For publicly traded companies, there is the daily stock price that gives the investing public's assessment of the trade-off between return and risk on a minute-by-minute basis. Small businesses do not have the luxury (or is it an advantage) of having the investing public continuously giving an appraisal of the company's risk through their trading activity and setting of the stock's price.

Performing a risk analysis for a small business is particularly difficult if the business does not have a long track record. Without a significant operating history and only limited historical financial results to track changes in the business variables and how those variables change as market conditions change, can make performing a meaningful risk analysis quite difficult. For a new small business, particularly one that is implementing a novel business idea, conducting an accurate risk assessment is not even reasonable. The best that one can do in such situations is to use some creativity in performing scenario analysis.

One way of getting a handle on the risks of a small business is to assume that the business will have similar risks to other small businesses in the same industry. Looking at the sensitivity of sales and expenses for other similar small companies in relation to the economy provides a sense of the level of risk.

A measure of the risk of bankruptcy is given by the Altman Z-Score. Derived by finance professor and bankruptcy expert Edward Altman, the Altman Z-Score provides a measure by which the probability of bankruptcy of a business can be determined.[4] A Z-Score above 2.99 implies that there is little chance of financial distress. Conversely, a Z-Score below 1.80 implies that there is a decent probability of bankruptcy. A Z-Score

---

[4]E. Altman. September, 1968. "Financial Ratios, Discriminant Analysis and the Prediction of Corporate Bankruptcy," *Journal of Finance* 23, no. 4, pp. 189–209.

between 1.80 and 2.99 is indeterminate. The Altman Z-Score is given by the following formula[5]:

$$Z\text{-Score} = 1.2 \times F_1 + 1.4 \times F_2 + 3.3 \times F_3 + 0.6 \times F_4 + 0.999 \times F_5$$

Where:

$$F_1 = \frac{\text{Current Assets - Current Liabilities}}{\text{Total Assets}}$$

$$F_2 = \frac{\text{Retained Earnings}}{\text{Total Assets}}$$

$$F_3 = \frac{\text{Earnings Before Interest and Taxes}}{\text{Total Assets}}$$

$$F_4 = \frac{\text{Market Value of Equity}}{\text{Book Value of Debt}}$$

$$F_5 = \frac{\text{Sales}}{\text{Total Assets}}$$

For Lake Ridge Winery for 20X3, the Altman Z-Score is as follows[6]:

$$Z\text{-Score} = 1.2 \times \frac{(444,088 - 103,490)}{3,309,893} + 1.4 \times \frac{118,463}{3,309,893}$$

$$+ 3.3 \times \frac{294,786}{3,309,893} + 0.6 \times \frac{1,618,463}{1,587,940} + 0.999 \times \frac{2,327,412}{3,309,893}$$

Altman Z Score = 1.74

---

[5]There have been several revisions to the Altman Z-Score but they are proprietary models that are not in the public domain.

[6]In our fictitious example, Lake Ridge Winery is a private company and is not publicly traded. We thus substituted Book Value of Equity for Market Value of Equity. The Market Value of Equity is the total value of the outstanding shares of the company, or the price of the shares multiplied by the number of shares outstanding.

As the calculation shows, Lake Ridge Winery's Altman Z-Score is close to, but below the 1.80 threshold, and thus it would be considered a significant credit risk. However, Lake Ridge Winery is still a relatively new company and its financials are improving dramatically. If Lake Ridge Winery can maintain its current rate of growth in profitability, it will likely be considered a very good credit risk in just a few short years. Like all ratio analysis, the Altman Z-Score needs to be assessed in the context of the company. While it is an accurate average measure for a large collection of companies, individual companies will vary based on their specific circumstances.

Many banks and financial institutions will use the Altman Z-Score or something similar to assess the credit risk of a loan and determine credit terms. It is prudent that small business managers keep a close eye on this key bankruptcy risk metric.

Weighted Average Cost of Capital

An important metric for a business is its weighted average cost of capital, which is frequently just called the firm's WACC. The WACC is used in a couple of different contexts and as a measure in a couple of different ways. The first use is that it is, as its name implies, the weighted average cost of the financing or capital that has been invested in or loaned to the business. It is thus the weighted average of the cost of debt for the business (adjusted for the tax effects of debt financing) and the implied cost of the equity.

When financial stakeholders invest in a business, they expect to be compensated for the risk that they are taking. Both shareholders and creditors are taking the risk that they may not get their money back. They are also taking the risk that the timing of their returns may be uncertain and that they might have been able to earn better or more stable returns elsewhere. Investors who invest in higher risk companies expect to earn a higher return. Therefore, the cost, or the expected return, is directly related to the amount of the perceived risk of investing in the company. Shareholders are taking a larger risk than creditors as the timing of their investment returns is more uncertain, and thus shareholders generally expect a higher return than creditors. If potential shareholders do not foresee a return that is in line with their perceived level of risk, they will choose to not invest in the company. The WACC is thus a weighted measure of the perceived riskiness of the company.

The WACC is also used as a discount rate to account for the time value of money. We will encounter this use of the WACC in Chapters 8 and 9.

The WACC is calculated as shown in Equation 4.1.

$$\text{WACC} = \text{Percentage of Debt} \times \text{Cost of Debt} \times (1 - \text{Tax Rate})$$
$$+ \text{Percentage of Equity} \times \text{Cost of Equity}$$

The percentage of Debt is simply the percentage of the long-term capital structure of the firm that is made up of debt. Likewise, the Percentage of Equity is the percentage of the long- term capital structure that is equity. We can thus rewrite the WACC formulas as in Equation 4.2.

$$\text{WACC} = \frac{\text{Total Long Term Liabilities}}{\text{Total Long Term Liabilities} + \text{Total Equity}}$$
$$\times \text{Cost of Debt} \times (1 - \text{Tax Rate})$$
$$+ \frac{\text{Total Equity}}{\text{Total Long Term Liabilities} + \text{Total Equity}}$$
$$\times \text{Cost of Equity} \tag{4.2}$$

The cost of the debt is simply the interest rate of the bank or debt financing multiplied by one minus the tax rate.[7] Determining the cost of equity for a private company is much more subjective. For publicly traded companies, there is a well-accepted methodology for calculating the appropriate cost of equity, which is based in part on the volatility of the publicly traded company's stock returns. Unfortunately, that approach is not suitable for a private company such as a small business.

The cost of equity should account for the riskiness or volatility of the cash flows. Small business owners generally do not directly take this risk into account and thus significantly underestimate their cost of equity.

---

[7] Interest on debt is tax deductible and thus the true cost of debt needs to be adjusted downward by the factor of one minus the tax rate to appropriately account for this tax deduction. Equity dividends are paid after taxes are calculated and thus do not have the same tax adjustment.

Some even believe that "sweat equity" is without cost, although this is obviously not true. Private equity companies and venture capitalists that specialize in investing in small businesses use a cost of equity that is significantly higher than the returns that they would earn from investing in the publicly traded stock markets to account for the enhanced risk of small businesses. At a minimum, the cost of equity should be at least a couple of percent higher than the cost of debt for the business.

To calculate the percentage of each type of financing, it can be assumed that the total long-term capital of the business is the sum of the Total Long-Term Liabilities and the Total Equity. This assumes that the Total Current Liabilities are being utilized to finance the Current Assets or the working capital of the firm. The percentage weightings should be based on the market values rather than the accounting or book values. Usually, the accounting value for debt is very similar to the market value. However, as pointed out in footnote 2 of Chapter 3, the market value of the equity is generally significantly different from the book value of the equity, and this is particularly true the longer the company has been in business.

Concluding Thoughts

Chapter 3 discussed the financial statements, while this chapter focused on how to interpret the financial statements. While financial statements are useful by themselves, the reality is that many of the external stakeholders of the business will use the data in the financial statements to make comparisons with the data of other companies that they deal with and with that of other investment possibilities. Ratio analysis is what enables different companies to be compared with each other on a reasonable basis. As ratio analysis is so important to the stakeholders of the firm, it is incumbent on the small business manager to understand how to perform and interpret a financial analysis. Doing so will give the business manager clues as to how their business is performing, how to improve it, and how to better deal with external stakeholders.

CHAPTER 5

Financial Forecasting and Planning

Failing to plan is planning to fail. Financial forecasting and planning is a necessity for the small business manager who wants to avoid the stress and inefficiencies of managing a business by reacting to one crisis after another. With the possible exception of planning at the initial stages of start-up, financial planning is the one financial activity that is often ignored or completed at the last minute on an as-needed basis. Ironically, the planning for marketing, the planning for staffing needs, and the planning for building the size and scope of operations are often frequently completed, but the financial planning, which makes each and every one of these activities possible, is either left out or at best left until last. Additionally, the financial planning needs are often incomplete and look at just one aspect of the business, while not realizing that financing is by necessity a holistic activity.

We separate the financial forecasting from the financial planning in a rather arbitrary way. We do so to point out that there are two specific tasks in preparing the financial plan of a business for the future. The first is forecasting forward the variables that affect the performance of the firm. This includes forecasting the sales, the expenses as well as the underlying economic variables that will affect the drivers of the firm's performance. The planning component is then putting those forecasts together into a projection of the financial results for the firm and testing the appropriateness of various financial strategies. This usually results in a few iterations of adjusting plans and using the new plans to forecast again with an alternate set of managerial influenced assumptions, until an appropriate set of plans has evolved.

Generally, forecasting and planning are considered to be one and the same, but we believe that explicitly breaking them down into two separate components, the nature and the importance of the tasks can be better realized. Having said that, we realize that it is a somewhat arbitrary separation, and thus we will frequently treat the two as one task.

In this chapter we cover the basics of short-term forecasting and planning as well as long-term forecasting and planning. Additionally, we discuss the very important role that developing forecasting scenarios as well as forecasting sensitivity analysis plays, given the uncertain nature of small business operations.

Why Financial Planning and Forecasting Is Important

Before looking at some of the specific issues of forecasting and planning it is useful to examine some of the reasons why taking the time and effort of going through a formal forecasting and planning exercise is so important as well as useful.

Understand the Amount of Capital Needed

The primary purpose for a financial forecast and plan is to understand the amount of financing that the business needs to carry out its operational plan. Particularly when it comes to expansion, or to capital budgeting projects, managers are quite good at tallying the amount needed for equipment, but much less so when it comes to the financing needs for human resources and working capital. Proper financial forecasting highlights explicitly the need for sufficient working capital and appropriate staffing levels that, although secondary, are still necessary and thus need to be financed appropriately.

Provide Insight into the Business Model

A financial forecast provides a wonderful amount of insight into how a business generates positive cash flows and profits for the business. In the process of developing a financial forecast, the manager is forced to explicitly consider all of the moving parts of the business and how they link together. This is especially so as subsequent forecasts are completed after learning about the mistakes and omissions of previous forecasts.

Aid Financial Backers in Understanding the Business

A well-constructed financial forecast and financial plan will not only help the business manager understand their business, but will also aid financial backers in their understanding. Potential investors and creditors, such as bankers, are much more likely to provide funds to a business, and to provide those funds on more favorable terms, the greater their understanding of the business. This does not mean that the forecast should be overly optimistic, or biased. Savvy financial backers will be able to quickly see through such bias and it will quickly sour them on both the business and the management. However, well-constructed and thought out forecasts that include realistic scenario analysis are a great aid to securing financing.

Provide Confidence to Financial Backers

In addition to helping financial backers understand the business, a well-constructed financial forecast provides confidence in the management of the business. One of the surest ways to lose the backing of a potential investor is to seek an amount of capital that is insufficient to carry out the intended operational strategy. Savvy investors, which by the way are the best type of investors to have in your small business, will have the insight to assess whether the financing requested is adequate. Most of these savvy investors would rather have the manager ask for excess funds, and have a reserve for contingencies, than not ask for enough and have to scramble to find additional financing as the need arises. A well-constructed financial forecast as part of the investment ask gives the potential investor confidence that the manager understands the business and understands how to operate it. A related point is that a well-constructed financial plan also helps to guide the difficult conversations that will ensue if the business fails to perform as expected and additional financing is needed.

Integrate the Financial Plan into the Operational Plan

A small business needs to be fully integrated. Departments do not have the luxury of working as silos; this of course does not even work well for large corporations. A financial forecast will integrate the various functions of the business and provide the various managers a common ground of understanding. Even if the business is simply a one-person operation, a financial forecast provides a framework for that manager to smoothly manage the business in an integrated manner.

Learn Where There Is Slack and Where There Are Constraints

A proper financial forecast will show where the business is operating at its limits and where there is room for growth. For instance, if growth in sales is desired, the financial should indicate whether or not there is sufficient working capital on hand and the processing capabilities are sufficient to provide enough product to meet the sales target. Likewise, it should highlight where there is slack, such as excess cash or spare production capacity beyond what is needed for manufacturing variances.

Test Alternative Plans and Strategies

An extremely useful application of a financial forecast is to test the reasonableness as well as the financial results of alternative operating plans and strategies. For example, should the business maintain a slow but steady growth strategy or undertake a quantum leap in scope and scale to build market share? A financial forecast can help to assess the advantages and disadvantages of alternative strategies such as these.

Learn the Key Metrics for Managing the Business

A financial plan combined with the appropriate scenario analysis and sensitivity analysis will provide valuable input for managing the business and alert the manager to the key value drivers. For example, if a sensitivity analysis shows changing the selling price by 1 percent changes the net profits by only a quarter of a percent but adjusting the variable administrative costs by 1 percent changes the profits by 5 percent, then it becomes obvious that the variable administrative costs deserve much more management attention than the selling price.

Understand the Key Risks of the Business

Related to learning about the key drivers of cash flow and profit for the business, the financial planning exercise will help the managers understand the key risk factors for the business. It will help to answer questions such as what will prevent the business from achieving its goals or what might happen that will push the business to surpassing its target objectives. Knowing the key risk factors is not simply good risk management, but also good management. Risk management is covered in Chapter 10.

Provide a Platform for Learning

Perhaps the most important reason to conduct a financial planning exercise on a regular basis is the learning that it provides about the business. Keeping a record of past financial forecasts, and comparing those forecasts with the actual achieved results, provides the small business manager a valuable learning opportunity. Learning about where prior forecasts were inaccurate not only improves the ability to build more accurate forecasts going forward, but also greatly provides information that can be used to manage the business more efficiently and effectively.

As will be further discussed later, financial forecasts are not reality nor will most financial forecasts turn out to be that accurate, and this is particularly so in the early stages of a business. That however does not invalidate the exercise of going through a financial forecasting and planning exercise. The exercise of financial forecasting itself has a lot of value to the business manager and can significantly improve the management of the business, regardless of whether it is particularly accurate or not. Thus, financial forecasting and planning should be done with a sense of humility about its accuracy, but also a keenness and respect for the managerial improvements it will bring.

The Life Cycle of Financial Planning

Every firm goes through a series of phases and the type of financial planning, as well as the significance of financial planning, changes as well. Generally speaking, there are five phases to the life of every business.

They are the Idea Phase, the Start-up Phase, the Development Phase, the Growth Phase, and the Maturity Phase. An additional phase is the Wind-up Phase, in which the business operator decides to exit the business.

The Idea Phase is when the business is nothing more than an idea in the head of the founders of the firm. The business is a concept and nothing more. Ironically this is where financial forecasting and a bit of financial planning can be most useful. Forecasting when the business is nothing more than a concept is obviously a very inaccurate exercise that is unlikely to produce any reasonably useful values. However, the discipline of financial planning, and of starting to make relationships between the financial variables that will affect the cash flows of the potential business, can help significantly into taking a fuzzy concept and being able to more concretely see how the parts might fit together. Having said that, it should be realized that, as with all parts of the planning at this concept stage, the plans are likely to be significantly, if not dramatically, altered before a single product is made or a single transaction completed.

The start-up phase is when the manager takes the concept and works to make it a viable product or service. Forecasting and planning at this stage is still likely to be more of an exercise in guessing than in anything concrete. The business model is likely to change significantly at this stage as the business model shifts as concepts are implemented, tested, and found wanting and in need of alterations. At this stage many businesses adopt a "lean start-up" philosophy, in which they attempt to create a "minimally viable product" and get it to potential customers as soon as possible in order to learn from the early customers' responses to the product, and alter the product or service accordingly.[1]

During the start-up phase, the key financial figure is the burn rate and the corresponding days cash on hand. The days cash on hand, discussed in Chapter 3, provides an estimate of the number of days that the company can survive without making a sale and without securing additional

---

[1] The "lean startup" was popularized in the book by E. Reis. 2011. *The Lean Startup: How Today's Entrepreneurs Use Continuous Innovation to Create Radically Successful Businesses* (New York, NY: Currency).

sources of financing. The days cash on hand provides the size of the window that the company has before it needs to generate positive cash flow through sales. An accurate forecast of this variable is crucial if the business is ever going to be successfully started.

The development phase is when the business starts to build routines and solidifies both its identity and it operating plan. The business is by no means mature, but it has some concepts that it knows will be successful, as well as some that it knows will not work in their current form. The development phase can be a bit of a trap phase for a business: The company has learned that it has a viable business model and thus may rest on its initial success. However, resting on its laurels at this time would be a serious mistake, as it is quite likely that the business will need to grow in order to achieve a sustainable level of success. Strategies for the business are being formed at this time, and if they are formed without significant forethought and testing of alternative strategies, the business may find itself locked into an inefficient and inflexible operating model that may prove very costly to it later. Financial planning at the development phase will ensure that the company has the financial flexibility and capacity to enter the next stage, the growth phase, of its development.

The growth phase of the business is where the needs for financial flexibility are probably the greatest. The irony is that many small businesses fail during the growth phase because they are too successful. Without adequate financing, in particular for the often-ignored working capital, a small business will quickly be killed by being unplanned for growth. Too much growth can paradoxically be even more toxic for a small business than too little growth. A proper financial forecast and financial plan at this stage, combined with adequate scenario analysis, will help a business avoid being financially strangled by its own success.

The maturity phase of the business is ultimately the goal of each small business operator. During the maturity phase the business has the luxury of defining its terms and operating according to a deliberate strategy. At the maturity phase, the business becomes more proactive to its market than reactive. It has achieved a level of operating success that it can ask such questions as does it remain a small business or does it attempt to branch out and grow in scale, scope geographically or in terms of expanded product lines and services.

The final phase of the business is the wind-up phase, in which the business is either sold as a working business or dismantled and sold in pieces. Even at the end of the business's life, financial forecasting and planning is useful as it provides important guidance on how the business should be valued if it is to be sold.

Just as there are phases to a business, there are phases to the financial planning cycle.

The first phase is the forecast of the variables that underlie the operations of the firm. During this phase the economics that affect the firm are determined and a reasonable forecast is made.

The second phase is to develop alternative financing strategies that can then be tested as to how they will perform in the long term.

The third stage is to adjust the plans until a plan is developed that will allow the business to achieve its business and strategic objectives.

The fourth stage is to implement the plan and the final stage is to watch the plan unfold and to learn how the plan is evolving and also to learn the lessons of what financial assumptions were valid and which were not. This learning of course will help inform and improve future forecasts.

Top-Down versus Bottom-Up Forecasting and Planning

A business is an intersection of its suppliers, its customers, its competitors, the general economy in addition to its own actions. A business does not exist in isolation and the financial forecast needs to take this into account. The variables that affect the success of the business are constantly changing, and the manager only has limited control over a few of the variables, namely, the actions of the business itself.

There are two main methods for forecasting: top-down and bottom-up. Top-down forecasting looks first at the broad economic factors, and from these broad economic factors, it forecasts how the economy will do, and in turn how the general economic outlook will affect the industry that the business operates in, and from that examines the likely actions of competitors, and only then develops the implications for the business itself.

Bottom-up forecasting focuses on what actions the business plans to implement and then from that basis tries to figure out, in order to determine the forecast, how suppliers, customers, and competitors will react.

Large multinational corporations generally invoke some form of long-range top-down forecasting. Large multinational companies tend to have very long planning cycles to counter the fact that they are not very nimble in their ability to react. This necessitates developing strategies that may takes years to fully implement.[2]

Small businesses are generally more local in their operations and in addition are more flexible in their operating strategies. This implies that planning need not be such an extensive exercise. However, given the nondiversified nature of small businesses, they need to be aware of the impacts of possible future outcomes as they may affect their survival. Small businesses will generally do a combination of top-down as well as bottom-up forecasting.

Local economic forecasts are generally readily available from the local chamber of commerce and are a great place to start developing an idea of the growth prospects for a business. In addition, many banks will publish economic forecasts for local regions as well. There are many local surveys available that mimic national surveys of business and consumer confidence.

Industry association groups are another excellent source for information on industry outlooks. Perhaps the best source of forecasting information comes from the business manager and their networking with suppliers, customers, and other similar businesses through trade groups and trade shows. The more knowledge that one has about how others are thinking, the better informed one is going to be in formulating their own forecast.

National economic statistics are frequently segmented by region. Major economic statistics that track the expected health of the economy include the Consumer Confidence Index and the Purchasing Managers Index, to name just two. The Consumer Confidence Index is published by the Conference Board and is a national survey of consumer optimism.[3] Likewise, the Purchasing Managers Index surveys businesses on their

---

[2] The classic reference on long-range forecasting and planning is the very readable book by P. Schwartz. 1996. *The Art of the Long View: Planning for the Future in an Uncertain World* (New York, NY: Currency).

[3] The Conference Board. 2020. "Consumer Confidence Survey®." https://www.conference-board.org/data/consumerconfidence.cfm.

intended level of supply purchases and is considered to be a key indicator of business confidence.[4] Other indices are available for specific industries. To supplement data collected by others, the business may wish to conduct their own survey, either formally or informally, among their suppliers or customers.

One of the most useful resources for planning is the company's own financial statements. Trends in the ratios that were discussed in Chapter 4 can give clues to the drivers of the business performance and how they react in different economic environments. In particular, the company's Common Size Income Statement and Common Size Balance Sheet are key in developing the pro-forma financial statements that are developed in the next section.

Forecasts generally begin with an estimate for the sales growth of the business. Basically, expected sales forms the basis for everything else that the business does, and it is also one of the reasons why the Common Size Income Statements were based off Revenue. After the sales growth forecast has been made, the assets required will have to be estimated. Again, having the Common Size Balance Sheet based on Total Assets aids in determining these values, as does the various efficiency ratios discussed in Chapter 4.

How often a firm does forecasting and planning, and how far forward into the future, is quite subjective and depends on the specific context of the business. Generally, a firm will want to have a reasonably robust forecast for the next year, as well as a general forecast for 2 to 5 years. Generally, forecasting beyond 2 years can be very dubious at best. It also depends on the type of industry. Capital intensive businesses that involve long manufacturing lead times, and require significant expenditures on capital intensive equipment, will have a need for much longer term forecasts than a service-based business with mainly variable costs that can be easily adjusted.

---

[4] IHS Markit. n.d. "PMI™." https://ihsmarkit.com/products/pmi.html?utm_source= google&utm_medium=ppc&utm_campaign=PC12053&gasc_id= 698311035&gasc_label=5aK2CJ_I_7EBEPvC_cwC&gclid=EAIaIQobChMI5vzJ4c 7b5wIVipyzCh1-mQmzEAAYASAAEgJmjPD_BwE.

The seasonal cyclicality of the business is also a factor. A toy store, for instance, tends to have very clear seasons, with Christmas season often driving the results for the year. For such businesses, quarterly or even monthly forecasts might be called for, while a business that is more stable throughout the year, such as a corner store, might be able to justify simply having a quarterly or even annual forecast.

Financial Planning Tools

There are two main tools for financial planning: the cash budget and the creation of pro-forma financial statements.

The cash budget is generally a 12 to 18 month forecast of the cash inflows and the cash outflows expected of the firm. The cash budget is key for determining the amount of working capital financing needed. As a key element of working capital management, the creation of the cash budget is covered in detail in Chapter 7, on working capital management. As the cash budget is used mainly to forecast working capital needs, it is frequently the main tool for determining the size of the operating line of credit needed.

Pro-forma financial statements are a prediction of what the financial statements of the firm will look like if certain operating forecasts and objectives are met. Pro-forma financial statements are a key planning tool for the longer term financing and in particular the proportion of debt and equity that will be needed if the company is to achieve its operating objectives. The pro-forma financial statements, and their projection for longer term capital needs, complement the cash budget, which shows the need for shorter term or temporary financing.

To illustrate the construction of a set of pro-forma financial statements, we will develop the financial statements for Lake Ridge Winery for the year 20X4. The key elements needed for a pro-forma are the current financial statements, a projection of sales for the forthcoming year(s) of the forecast, and forecast values for the various line items that go into the make-up of the Income Statement and Balance Sheet of the business. The ratio analysis and the Common Size Income Statement and Balance Sheets that were developed in Chapter 4 are a major help in the construction of the pro-forma.

For the purposes of illustration, we are going to make the following assumptions for Lake Ridge Winery:

- Total Revenue is expected to increase 20 percent for year 20X4
- Wages and benefits will remain the same proportion of Total Revenues
- Purchases are expected to increase from 35 percent of Total Revenues to 37 percent
- Advertising and promotion expenses are expected to be $135,000 in order to support the aggressive Revenue goal
- The Management Fees will be maintained at a level of $200,000
- All other Operating Expenses, as well as Income Tax, are expected to have the same proportion of Total Revenue (as shown in the Common Size Income Statement) as they did for the previous year (20X3)

Proforma Income Statement - Lake Ridge Winery			
	20X3	Pro-forma 20X4	
Revenue			
Total Revenue	2,327,412	2,792,894	increased by 20%
Cost of sales			
Wages and benefits	163,695	196,434	same proprotion as before
Purchases	818,473	1,033,371	increased to 0.37 of Revenues
Total COGS	982,168	1,229,805	
Gross Profit	1,345,244	1,563,090	
Operating expenses			
Labour and commissions	426,981	512,377	same proprotion as before
Depreciation	156,457	187,748	same proprotion as before
Repairs and maintenance	47,852	57,422	same proprotion as before
Utilities and telecommunication	32,586	39,103	same proprotion as before
Interest and bank charges	138,228	165,873	same proprotion as before
Professional and business fees	44,221	53,065	same proprotion as before
Advertising and promotion	95,214	135,000	estimate for new advertising program
Delivery & shipping expenses	28,789	34,547	same proprotion as before
Insurance	18,358	22,030	same proprotion as before
Management fees	200,000	200,000	maintained at 200,000
Total Operating Expenses	1,188,686	1,407,166	
Income Before Tax	156,559	155,924	
Income Taxes	13,840	16,608	
Net Income	142,719	139,316	

Figure 5.1 Pro-forma income statement

With these assumptions, we can create the pro-forma Income Statement for 20X4 as shown in Figure 5.1.

A similar process can be done for the pro-forma Balance Sheet. To build the pro-forma Balance Sheet there are simply a couple of extra components to remember. The first is that the Net Income, or Net Income After Dividends, is carried over from the pro-forma Income Statement to the Equity Section of the Balance Sheet. You will recall from Chapter 3 that this is the linkage between the Income Statement and the Balance Sheet. The second component to building the pro-forma Balance Sheet is that we are going to leave the Bank Loan, as well as the Capital Stock, blank as a temporary measure. Later, we will use these two line items to determine the total amount of long-term financing needed by "balancing" the Balance Sheet. The third component to remember is that the Balance Sheet must balance, in that the Total Assets must be equal to the Total Liabilities and Equity.

To build the pro-forma Balance Sheet we will make the following assumptions:

- The Cash balance will be targeted to be $350,000
- Land and Building will remain the same, but Equipment will rise to $920,000 as new processing equipment to meet the increased sales target will be required
- To increase the sales, it is expected that the winery will have to extend credit to more customers and thus the Days Accounts Receivable are expected to rise to 20 days
- Days Inventory and Days Payables will all remain the same as they were for the previous year (Chapter 4 illustrates the calculation of these values as well as Days Account Receivable)
- All other Balance Sheet items (except Bank Loan, Capital Stock, and Current Year Earnings, which have been discussed) are expected to increase in proportion to Revenues (i.e., by 20 percent)

As can be seen from Figure 5.2, the Total Liabilities and Equity is $3,601,681. Total Current Liabilities, Other Long-Term Liabilities, Retained Earnings, and Current Year Earnings will make up $405,573 of this. This implies that the Bank Loan as well as the Capital Stock of the

	Proforma Balance Sheet Lake Ridge Winery		
		Pro-forma	
	20X3	20X4	
Assets			
Current Assets			
Cash	$365,138	$350,000	
Accounts Receivable	36,556	153,035	Increase to 20 Days of Account Receivable
Inventory	42,394	53,525	Same Days Inventory
Total Current Assets	444,088	556,560	
Fixed Assets			
Land	540,000	540,000	Unchanged
Building	2,093,226	2,093,226	Unchanged
Equipment	656,000	920,000	Expected to increase to $920,000
Accumulated Depreciation	(423,421)	(508,105)	Assumed to grow in proportion to Revenue
Total Net Fixed Assets	2,865,805	3,045,121	
Total Assets	3,309,893	3,601,681	
Liabilities & Equity			
Current Liabilities			
Accounts Payable	95,361	120,399	Same Days Payable
Accrued Liabilities	8,129	9,755	Assumed to grow in proportion to Revenue
Total Current Liabilities	103,490	130,154	
Long Term Liabilities			
Bank Loan	1,573,241	**	To be determined by financing decision
Other Long Term Liabilities	14,699	17,639	Assumed to grow in proportion to Revenue
Total Long Term Liabilities	1,587,940	**	To be determined by financing decision
Total Liabilities	1,691,430	**	To be determined by financing decision
Equity			
Capital Stock	1,500,000	**	To be determined by financing decision
Retained Earnings	(24,255)	118,464	From pro-forma Income Statement
Current Year Earnings	142,719	139,316	From pro-forma Income Statement
Total Equity	1,618,463	**	To be determined by financing decision
Total Liabilities & Equity	3,309,893	3,601,681	Must be same as Total Assets

Figure 5.2   Pro-forma Balance Sheet

business must be $3,196,108 ($3,601,681 minus $405,573). However, the existing total of the Bank Loan and Capital Stock is only $3,073,241, which means that the business needs to raise an additional $122,867 of financing if it is to achieve its operating objectives.

Scenario and Sensitivity Analysis

All forecasts are wrong. That is not necessarily a problem for the reasons that were discussed in an earlier section of this chapter. However, the reality is that one can never know the future. As such, the prudent manager takes advantage of the forecasting and planning and develops a variety of scenarios. In addition, they will do a related exercise in developing a sensitivity analysis.

Scenario analysis is simply developing different future scenarios and then examining how the financial results of the business would look under those alternative scenarios. At a minimum it is instructive to develop three base scenarios: a base case or expected case, a reasonably expected worst case scenario, and finally a reasonably expected best case scenario. These scenarios aid the manager in examining whether the company has enough slack and flexibility to manage such a range of possible outcomes.

Other "what-if" scenarios can be developed to develop contingency plans to avoid a negative outcome or to be able to exploit a potential special opportunity. Some businesses also develop a worst case scenario as part of their business survival planning. Knowing that the business can survive a worst case scenario greatly aids in downside risk management.

Sensitivity analysis is related to, but quite different from, scenario analysis in the information that it provides. In a scenario analysis a group of variables are changed at the same time to see what the outcomes are. A sensitivity analysis looks at changing each of the variables individually and then examining the change in outcomes. Obviously, variables do not change in isolation, so from that aspect the sensitivity analysis is a bit theoretical in its nature. However, what the sensitivity analysis does show is the relative importance of the various variables, and that is its value. For example, if changing sales growth by 1 percent changes expected Net Income by only a quarter of a percent in the forecast, but changing Total Asset Turnover by 1 percent changes Net Income by 5 percent in the forecast, then the manager knows that Total Asset Turnover is roughly 20 times more important for Net Income than sales growth. This provides valuable information to the manager as to where they should spend their limited time and energy in managing the business.

Both scenario analysis and sensitivity analysis are key for not only financial forecasting, but also for assessing capital budgeting projects and in developing cash budgets. Building forecasts and financial plans in spreadsheets makes scenario analysis and sensitivity analysis easy and quick to do. Scenario analysis and sensitivity analysis also help in the learning for the development of better plans and forecasts.

Forecasting and Planning Tips and Traps

The Plan Is a Model, Not Reality

Never mistake the plan for reality. All plans are simply a model at best, and a wildly incorrect guess at worst. When forecasting and planning, it is wise to have a measure of humility about the activity. Forecasting and planning should be viewed as much as an exercise in learning as it is an exercise in knowing. Having said that, with discipline and experience the accuracy of planning and forecasting will dramatically improve and in the process become much more valuable as an aid in managing the business.

Elegance Is for Tailors

Einstein is often given credit for the saying that elegance is for tailors. A more elegant, or a more sophisticated, forecast is not generally a better forecast or plan. The level of detail, or elegance, of the forecast should be in line with both the level of expected accuracy or ability to forecast and the actual level of complications that arise from business operations.

If a business is inherently volatile or difficult to develop an accurate forecast for, then a more detailed and involved planning model is not likely to improve the ability to foresee the future. In such cases, a more elegant model only leads to a false sense of knowledge.

In a similar vein, if the business itself is very simple, with a few variables and minimal factors that affect outcomes, then a very simple forecasting model is justified. A more elaborate model is simply extra work that does little to advance one's knowledge of the business or of how future possibilities might evolve.

Just When You Think It's a Trend You Find Out It's a Cycle

All forecasts to some extent are simply an extension of history, or a historical trend. However, business tends to occur in cycles. This is true for all levels, whether at the business level or at the local economic level, the national economic level or even the global economic level. Naively assuming trends will continue forever will likely only lead to nasty surprises. Businesses need to evolve and change as trends change. The planning and forecasting exercise, in conjunction with scenario and sensitivity analysis, should help in guiding the business to change as trends change, and indeed perhaps even to exploit trends for competitive advantage.

Life Is Not Linear Nor Is It Exponential

Likewise, trends, when they exist, are not always smooth, linear, or exponential. Even the most well behaved of trends will be anything but smooth. Indeed, there is always noise, or randomness, in the actual realized outcomes. By its very nature, one cannot predict randomness, and the best that one can do is get an estimate of the potential range of the randomness.

Also, many business forecasters get seduced by both linear as well as exponential growth. Nothing grows at the same pace forever, and this is particularly true for exponential growth. The early growth values of the business are highly likely to continue forever, despite how much it might be desired for them to do so.

Black Swans and Paradigm Shifts

A Black Swan is a highly unlikely event that has a very large impact. The terrorist attack on the World Trade Center of September 11, 2001, is an example of a Black Swan. The attacks were something that no one foresaw as a practical occurrence, yet the outcome of that day significantly affected almost everyone.

By definition, Black Swan events are very difficult to predict or to plan for. The best that one can do is hope that the business is flexible and quick enough to mitigate, survive, or exploit as appropriate the event or events should they occur.

Likewise, paradigm shifts occur. Apple's iTunes very rapidly changed the music industry, but within a decade, iTunes has become almost irrelevant as streaming services have become the dominant paradigm. Virtually no business or industry is immune from paradigm shifts.

Forecasting and planning cannot predict Black Swans nor are they particularly helpful in predicting paradigm shifts. However, having forecasting and planning discipline can significantly help a business to recognize when either a Black Swan or a paradigm shift has occurred, and likewise can provide ideas about how the future can evolve. Thus, while forecasting as an exercise is useless about prediction of such events, it is indispensable for helping to manage in such situations.

The Goal Should Be Based on the Forecast

Finally, the goal, or objective, for the business should be based on the forecast and not the other way around. Too often a business will set a goal—for growth, for instance—and then develop forecast scenarios that fit that goal. This is setting the forecast on the basis of the goal and is a common trap and a huge mistake. Businesses need to make a forecast first, and then and only then, determine what goals or objectives are reasonable. Forecasting and planning is not an exercise to justify inappropriate objectives; it is an exercise to develop appropriate objectives.

Concluding Thoughts

General Eisenhower reportedly once said, "In times of war, planning is indispensable; plans are useless." When it comes to small businesses, we for the most part heartily agree with his quote. Forecasting and planning will not necessarily give you an accurate picture of what the future holds but forecasting and planning is essential if a business is to be ready for whatever does happen.

Forecasting and planning is a tool and a discipline. Forecasting and planning does not determine the decisions the manager needs to make, but it does most certainly inform those decisions. Furthermore, forecasting and planning is a key element in learning about the business and building knowledge of the key drivers and how the important variables affect outcomes.

While forecasting and planning may seem like just an extra task for the business manager, we are highly confident that it is a task that will pay big dividends if thoughtfully attended to.

CHAPTER 6

Financial Management and Financing

In the previous five chapters we have discussed some of the concepts and analytics of financial management. In this chapter we start the discussion of the actual financing of the firm and the implementation of the major decisions of the financial manager. However, before beginning the decisions regarding financing, it is useful to develop a framework that ties together the different types of financial decisions.

A Framework for Financial Decision Making

In Chapter 2 we discussed how finance is the management of the trade-offs between return and risk, or more appropriately, between cash flow and risk. If the business managers are solely concerned about financial wealth, then this would be where the decisions regarding trade-offs would end. However, we continued the discussion to discuss the importance of the other objectives that small business owners as well as managers have. We thus discussed at length the importance of maximizing utility and how maximizing utility can be quite different from maximizing wealth. In this chapter we introduce the major types of financial decisions that the small business manager needs to deal with on a regular basis. We begin by introducing a framework for putting these financial decisions into the context of the overall objectives of the business.

There are four major categories of decisions for the small business manager. They are capital budgeting, choosing financing, working capital management, and risk management.

Capital budgeting is deciding what to spend money on in terms of investment. Capital budgeting is also about making the tough decision of what not to spend money on. In essence, capital budgeting involves trade-offs and prioritization, as most small businesses do not have the resources, financial or otherwise, to pursue all of the attractive capital budgeting opportunities that are available to them. Capital budgeting will be discussed in Chapter 8.

The second task involves financing, which is the main subject of this chapter. Financing is making choices for the sources of capital for the company that it will use to finance its investments in capital budgeting as well as in working capital management.

Working capital management is managing the day-to-day cash flows and operational activities of the firm. Working capital management includes tasks as diverse as ensuring cash is on hand to meet payroll through to developing credit strategies for customers. Working capital management will be covered in Chapter 7.

Risk management is deciding the level of risk, both financial risk and operational risk, that the business should have and implementing measures and tactics to ensure that the business operates at a risk level that is close to its risk objective. Risk Management is the topic of Chapter 10.

To put these decisions into context we have created a framework to illustrate the integration of these decisions that is illustrated in Figure 6.1.[1]

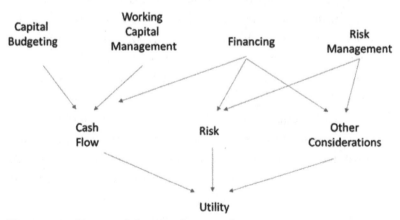

Figure 6.1   Financial decision framework

[1]This framework was loosely inspired by the Corporate Value Framework outlined in E.F. Brigham, M.C. Ehrhardt, J. Gessaroli, and R.R. Nason. 2017. *Financial Management: Theory and Practice* (3rd Canadian ed., Toronto, Canada: Nelson Education).

The bottom of the framework illustrates the ultimate objective of the financial manager: maximize utility. The three components that feed into the utility of the business are (1) the cash flows of the business, (2) the risk of the business, and (3) the other considerations of the business, which would include the utility objectives of the small business manager.

Decisions about capital budgeting as well as working capital management mainly affect the cash flows. Choices made in how the business is financed however have the most impact on the risk of the company, and in particular, the financial risk. Finally, decisions regarding the risk management of the firm affect not only the risk, but also the other considerations of the business. Admittedly, each of the types of financial decisions will have an effect on each of the components, either directly or directly, but the framework shows the most significant linkages.

The critical point to realize is that financial decisions are interrelated to each other. They are also intertwined with the other operational decisions of the business. It should go without saying that financial decisions have an impact on the operations, the marketing, the employees, the shareholders and creditors, and all of the other stakeholders of the firm. Thus, financial decisions cannot be made in isolation. The aforementioned framework is an attempt to put the connectedness of financial decisions into an understandable and simple context.

Considerations for Financing

There are many sources of potential financing for the small business. Choosing among the many possible choices can be tricky. However, the particular form of financing chosen at a given point in time can have significant implications in the short term, and especially, in the long-term level of success of the business. Unfortunately, many small business managers simply pick the most convenient or the most readily available form of financing without exploring the full set of possibilities.

A more comprehensive financing decision will take into account these factors: cost, availability, effort to secure and maintain financing, flexibility or restrictions of financing, control issues, tax implications, risk, and even the signaling effect. For the small business owner an additional factor is also relevant, namely, the understandability of the form of financing.

Cost

Cost of financing is an obvious consideration. All else being equal, the lower the cost of financing, the better. Later in this chapter we will discuss the WACC. The WACC is exactly what its name says, it is the weighted cost of financing of all the sources of financing for the firm. It is important for two reasons. The first is that the lower the cost of financing, the greater the net residual benefits will be to the shareholders or owners of the business. The second benefit is that the lower the WACC, the greater the value of the firm will be, all else being equal.

The cost of the financing can sometimes be tricky to calculate. For instance, what is the cost of the owner's sweat equity? It is certainly not zero, for if the owner were not putting time into building the business, they could probably earn an income working for someone else. The time spent building the business through sweat equity could productively be spent earning wages. The cost of sweat equity must account for not only the forgone wages, but also for the stress and worry that the business proprietor takes upon themselves. Counteracting this might be the joy of working for one's self rather than working for another person or a corporation.

Even the cost of a bank loan with a stated interest rate can be tricky to evaluate as covenants on the loan or restrictions, such as mandatory balances, can be a source of hidden fees and costs. These fees should definitely be included when considering the cost of the capital.

Furthermore, the tax implications of various types of financing need to be taken into account. While one should never choose a form of financing simply for the tax implications, the reality is that certain forms of financing, such as debt, have beneficial tax effects that can significantly lower the tax bill.

A more holistic view of cost of financing is required. The cost of financing needs to be taken into account with the overall objectives of the business. For instance, if a major objective is to grow rapidly, then growing financing needs are likely and thus flexibility to scale the financing may be a more critical factor than cost. While lower cost in financing is preferred, that is only true when all else is equal, and when it comes to sources of financing, the reality is that all else being equal is generally not the case when it comes to cost.

Availability

Availability is generally a key concern for a small business, and especially so when they are in the start-up phase and do not have a sufficient enough of a track record to attract traditional sources of financing, such as bank loans.

Hunting down sources of financing is generally not the most fun activity for the manager of a small business. In essence it can often seem like going begging with hat in hand. Thus, it is only natural that the most available source of funds is generally the source that is used first. Even for large publicly traded corporations that have investment bankers constantly pitching financing ideas to them, there is a strong tendency to use the most available sources of financing first.

The problem of course is that the most available source of financing is generally not the best source of financing for a variety of reasons. For example, internally generated funds, namely, the retained earnings of the firm, are readily available for use. However, if these funds are depleted for capital expenditures, then the business will be left with little to no financial flexibility, and additionally, will be relying on the patience of its shareholders for dividends, which may in the long run discourage these and other investors from contributing more funds to the business. Also, the true cost of retained earnings is generally quite high when properly costed out compared with other sources of financing.

It is an often-stated truism that the small business manager always has to be selling, even when they have all the orders that they can handle. The financing equivalent of this is that the small business manager should always be searching for sources of financing, even when they currently have all of the financing that they need. Relying on the most available sources of financing is a risky strategy that has a high probability of negatively costing the business in the long run.

Effort to Secure and Maintain Financing

Often related to the availability of financing is the effort required to secure a given source of financing. Some forms of financing are simply a hassle to not only secure, but to also maintain. For instance, some banks or external financiers or granting agencies may require an onerous amount of paperwork to be maintained. While in many cases this paperwork has a good reason for its being, and indeed may be analysis that is as much for the benefit of the business manager as it is for the financing source, the reality is that at times it may detract from the operation of the business.

Flexibility or Restrictions of Financing

Flexibility of financing should be a major financing consideration. For instance, bank loans or loans from external investors may contain restrictive covenants to protect the interests of the investor over those of the business owner. Covenants come in two generic forms. Positive covenants are items that the company must do in order to keep the loan in good order. Examples of positive covenants might include buying keyperson insurance or maintaining a minimum cash balance in the bank. Negative covenants are items that the business is not allowed to do. Examples include paying more than a given percentage of profits as dividends to shareholders or seeking other forms of financing without prior approval.

Flexibility issues also extend beyond covenants. Flexibility in financing also implies a diversity of funding sources. When one source of financing dries up, such as happened in the short-term debt markets after the 2008 recession, having flexibility in financing is crucial. By developing a portfolio of different sources of financing, the business develops a natural hedge against one source of financing potentially becoming dry or unavailable. Developing several sources of financing involves developing relationships across different stakeholder sectors. This of course requires work, but in the long run will likely pay benefits as it gives the firm flexibility, greater assurance of being able to finance, and also helps the manager to learn the advantages and disadvantages of the different sources of financing as they relate to their specific business.

Control Issues

When issuing equity, the business proprietor is in essence selling a portion of the business to others. This has advantages in that it shares the risk among the new shareholders, but also the disadvantage of losing at least partial, if not total, control of the business.

For some managers, the issue of control may not be a major issue. For many small business managers however it is a huge issue. For this reason, debt type instruments are preferred, and while money from an equity-seeking investor, such as a venture capitalist, may be very tempting, many small businesses will opt to grow more slowly in order to avoid bringing in external equity partners.

Like all of the issues of financing, control involves trade-offs and difficult choices. The issue of how much control (if any) to give up for financing is generally one of the toughest factors to decide upon. This is where having a clear objective for the business is key. The strategic objectives should drive the financing, not the other way around.

Tax Implications

Taxes are a fundamental cost of doing business, and all else being equal, reducing taxes will benefit the business. (This of course assumes that the business is producing profits and thus is in a taxable position.)

All else being equal, interest bearing sources of financing will be more tax efficient than equity bearing sources. This of course is due to the tax deductibility of interest payments versus the fact that dividends payments are made on an after-tax basis.

Risk

Various forms of financing have different levels of risk. For instance, we saw in Chapter 2 how adding debt increases the financial risk of the business. Debt also increases the risk of bankruptcy, which has its own involved costs. Different forms of financing also help to spread the risk. For instance, equity financing is essentially spreading the risk of failure among a group of equity investors, as the comments on the signaling consideration make clear.

Generally speaking, the lower the risk to the investor, the lower the cost of financing. From the investor's point of view, debt is considered to be of less risk than investing with equity. This is because debt investors can put covenants on the firm's actions. Debt holders also demand a steady stream of interest payments, while dividend payments are discretionary, and such dividend payments act as an early warning signal that the business is running out of cash if they are not paid in a timely fashion. Additionally, debt investors will get paid first in the event of a liquidation and may also have specific assets pledged as collateral. For all these reasons, debt financing is generally less expensive than equity financing.

The lower risk to the investor means that debt is a higher risk form of financing from the business's point of view. Debt means that the margin of error for losing control to the debt holders is lower. Increased levels of debt increase the risk of bankruptcy, which itself is costly in that it involves significant legal fees. Even an enhanced probability of bankruptcy can be costly even though the business remains financially solid. An enhanced threat of bankruptcy may drive customers away as they will not want to purchase from a company that may not be around to offer support to their products. An enhanced threat of bankruptcy will also influence suppliers, who may change their credit terms. Additionally, as bankruptcy risk increases, so does the cost of all other sources of financing, including any debt. Finally, an increased risk of bankruptcy will affect the way the managers do business, as key employees may leave for more stable companies, or market opportunities for growth may be forgone due to the limited flexibility that near bankruptcy may bring. A key cost of near bankruptcy may be the stress that it puts on the managers of the business. The important point is that a firm does not need to actually go bankrupt for the risk of bankruptcy to be a significant factor in the overall operations.

Signaling

If you knew for certain that your business was going to be a smashing success, would you want to share the outstanding profits with other, perhaps unknown shareholders? Conversely, if you knew that the outcomes for your business were iffy, would you want to risk everything you own on its success? In that iffy case, would you not want to share some of the downside risk?

This is the basis of what is known as the "signaling effect." Proprietors who are highly confident that their business is going to be a huge success will tend to seek out forms of financing in which they will retain as much control over the profits and retain as much of the risk as possible. Conversely, proprietors of businesses where the prospects are much more uncertain will tend to seek out sources of financing where they can share some of the downside risk and put less of their own equity in jeopardy.

Understandability

A final consideration for the small business manager is the understandability of the financing. The optimal form of financing is anything but optimal if the manager does not understand it and has to spend energy fretting about it, or even worse, is blindsided by an unknown or misunderstood implication of the financing.

Some forms of financing may be so complicated that special expertise, such as legal or accounting advice, may need to be purchased. Not only does this entail an explicit cost of specialist fees, but also involves management time and energy to deal with.

Debt versus Equity

There are many different choices for financing, which we will discuss shortly. In broad terms though, all sources of financing can be roughly classified into the two categories of debt and equity. In generic terms, debt involves a finite loan of funds that require mandatory periodic interest payments and repayment of the funds at a specific time or set of times. Other terms may be involved with debt financing as well, such as covenants. Equity financing however involves an ownership share in the business, with a discretionary payment of dividends.

Although the direct costs of equity are conceptually nonexistent as the business gets to decide whether or not and how much to pay as a dividend to the shareholders, the reality is that debt is generally an overall lower cost of financing. Equity shareholders will not maintain their investment in the business unless their return justifies it, and thus equity financing will dry up unless there is clear evidence that the equity investors are being suitably compensated for their increased level of risk.

The choice between debt and equity financing is the classic finance trade-off between risk and return. Equity involves lower risk and lower constraints for the business, but a higher cost. There is no one right or optimal answer for the proportional mix of debt and equity. They each have their advantages as well as their disadvantages; it truly is a classic set of trade-offs. One aspect that does appear to be clear is that extremes in the amount of either debt or of equity tend to be suboptimal. There appear to be clear advantages to the firm having at least some debt and at least some equity in their capital structure.

It should be pointed out that the capital structure of a firm will likely evolve. In fact, it is likely that even the most carefully run businesses will be constantly adjusting their capital structure. First, this is due to the fact that financing is a "bulky" activity, that is, you cannot finance in small and precise amounts, but generally need to get a chunk of financing at a time. Second, businesses will change their mix of financing as they mature and change their product and sales mix. Finally, businesses will also change their capital structure in anticipation of changes in their market or anticipated changes in their operating strategies.

Long-Term versus Short-Term Financing

After deciding upon the mixture of debt and equity, the next broad financing decision is the mix of short-term versus long-term debt. A general rule of thumb is to finance long-term assets with long-term debt and short-terms assets with a short-term form of financing. For instance, a business might finance their building and plant with a mortgage loan, but their seasonal inventory expenses with a seasonal operating line of credit.

Other considerations in terms of short-term versus long-term financing are cost, flexibility, and risk. Generally long-term financing is more expensive than short-term financing. The trade-off is that longer term financing is less risky and provides more flexibility. It is less risky as the financing is already secured and obtained. If the business gets into financial difficulty, it may become difficult for it to obtain financing. Additionally, as many businesses experienced during the recession of 2008, downturns in the economy may make obtaining any form of financing more expensive. Finally, short-term rates tend to fluctuate or have more volatility than long-term rates.

One of the considerations as well is the cyclicality of the need for financing. As a business grows, their overall need for financing also tends to grow. However, on top of this growing trend for greater financing there may be a cyclicality of financing needs. The classic example would be that of a toy shop that needs financing to build inventory for the critical Christmas season. However, after Christmas such a business is usually flush with cash—in October and November the need for financing is great, while in January the need for financing is much less. This creates a financing dilemma. If the firm obtains long-term financing to cover their needs for October and November, they will have excess cash in January and excess financing on which they are paying an interest rate that will only be partially covered by the interest earned on their excess cash. Conversely, if they choose to finance seasonally with short-term financing, they will have to annually seek seasonal financing, which may be difficult or costly due to changing market conditions.

Obtaining long-term financing to meet peak expected needs for several years will generally be more costly, but the financing will be secured; the interest rate, assuming it is fixed, will be known; and the manager does not need to worry about a seasonal rush to obtain financing and can focus their energy on other parts of the business. The excess cash can be invested in short-term investments to help offset the excess financing charges. This is a conservative yet expensive strategy. Conversely, a mix of short-term and long-term financing can be used, which will be less expensive but require seasonal effort to obtain short-term financing.

Finally, some businesses opt for a very aggressive and risky strategy by financing all of their needs with short-term financing. This has the advantage of being generally less expensive as only short-term financing is used, and it will be easier to forecast the amount of short-term financing needed and thus the firm will not be borrowing more than is needed. However, this strategy involves a constant need to seek financing which can be time consuming for management; it may also backfire if market conditions drive the short-term rates higher or make the financing unavailable. This was the case for many companies using this strategy at the time of the 2008 recession, and they suffered greatly, with many being forced to go out of business, while companies that had followed the more costly, but less risky longer term financing strategy, were able to weather the storm.

Another significant risk with this short-term financing strategy is that the health of the business may go through a rough patch. If this happens, the business may be unable to secure even short-term financing at competitive rates. Thus, just when the business needs financing the most, it may be unattainable. Having secured long-term financing, a business is more sheltered from short-term effects such as downturns in the business cycle. Long-term financing allows a business to weather down cycles and survive until business conditions improve.

Types of Financing

As the previous sections discuss, there are a number of factors to consider when choosing a form of financing. To complicate matters there are almost as many different sources and forms of financing. In this section we will discuss some of the more common types for small businesses. Note however that this is not an exhaustive list as the types and forms of financing are too numerous to list.

Self-Financing

Self-financing, or owner financing, may be one of the most common forms of financing for start-up businesses. There are several advantages in that the owner retains complete control and is not subject to any of the hassles that may come about when dealing with other forms of financing. The downside is that the financing is generally very limited, which restricts the potential growth of the business. It is also very risky in that the owner is taking all of the economic effect if the business fails. This of course adds to the stress levels of what can already be a stressful environment.

Bootstrapping

Closely related to self-financing is bootstrapping, in which the initial cash flows of the firm are used to finance its growth. While conceptually ideal, the reality is that few businesses can generate positive cash flows quickly enough to sustain themselves.

While on the topic of bootstrapping, it should be mentioned that using retained earnings is not a free form of financing. Yes, the cash flows generated by the firm are available and do not charge an explicit interest rate, but exhausting internally generated funds to finance the business means that dividends are not being paid to existing shareholders, which in turn may discourage them from investing more into the business. Also, exhausting internally generated funds for ongoing operations limits the flexibility of the firm for those instances when a readily available source of cash will allow it to take advantage of special opportunities.

Friends and Family

After using personal funds, sourcing financing from friends and family may be one of the most common sources of new venture financing. Family and friends financing has the same advantages and disadvantages of self-financing. However, there is the additional concern of dealing with the stress of putting the resources of acquaintances at risk, and the potential long-term negative consequences of this such as strained personal relationships even if things go well with the business and a sufficient return is generated for the investors. The numerous well-publicized squabbles of family owned firms are testament to the hazards of too much reliance on this form of financing.

The general rule of thumb that financial planners give to investors who are considering providing Friends and Family type financing to a family member is to mentally consider the money to be a gift. If a return is generated, then it is a bonus, but if the money is lost then there should be no hard feelings as it was mentally considered to be a gift and thus no return was expected. The personal emotional issues with Friends and Family financing make this a prudent way to think about this as an as a type of investment.

Social Media

Social media platforms are a recent form of financing a small business. Social media sites, such as Kickstarter, provide a forum for a small business to raise money from the general public. In certain cases, the financing may come from enthusiasts who are interested in purchasing the products that the business is developing. The financing may be structured as either equity or as debt, which is generally referred to as "peer-to-peer lending."

Although the concept of "crowdfunding" has been around for basically as long as entrepreneurial ventures, the rise of the Internet and the ubiquity of social media are dramatically changing the landscape for this type of financing and creating a new set of issues. Currently most social funding is for project-based ventures, but as the concept develops and as the legal issues with the structure also develop, this could conceivably quickly become a major source of small business financing.

Angel Investors

Angel investors are a very important part of the financing infrastructure for small businesses. Angel investors are nonassociated third-party investors who specialize in making relatively modest equity (or sometimes debt structured) investments in small businesses. Angel investors have been popularized by the hit television show *Shark Tank*. Angel investors may be individuals or a group of individuals who have pooled their personal money to make high-risk investments in small businesses and start-ups.

Angel investors are generally experienced entrepreneurs and small business creators themselves, so they understand the risks, but also the potential upsides of such businesses. As they are taking a lot of risk, they generally expect to earn very healthy returns and generally a sizeable stake in the business. Conversely, they also expect that they will lose money on most of the investments that they make.

The advantage of having angel investors is that, in addition to their financing, they will also be able, and in fact may demand, to provide some valuable experience and guidance. Successful angel investors will also generally have an extensive list of contacts and connections that they can call on for help on specific tasks needed to help develop a small business. Some small business owners may not welcome the help, but in the vast majority of cases, the advice and assistance of an angel investor should be enthusiastically welcomed. It must be noted that although an angel investor will provide assistance on an occasional basis, they are not expecting to have to regularly step in to provide management assistance.

Venture Capital

Venture capitalists are a more formalized and structured form of angel investor. Like an angel investor, a venture capitalist invests in relatively early stage businesses. Unlike an angel investor, they are investing money that has been raised from outside investors. They also prefer to only invest in businesses that have a proven product and an established customer base. Therefore, a venture capitalist generally comes in to invest in a business after it has achieved a scale that is beyond the scope of what the angel investor is able to provide.

A venture capitalist is likely to take a much more active form in the management of the business. It is quite common for a venture capital firm to insist on installing their own managers into key roles and positions in the business. While this provides the business with expertise, it might also greatly restrict the amount of control that the business originators have.

A further aspect of a venture capitalist is that they do not want to tie their money up in the business into perpetuity. They will want to realize a return on their capital invested by eventually taking the business public or selling the business to a larger company. This is another way that the control of the original owner is significantly compromised when venture capital investment is sought.

Government Sponsored Financing and Grants

Small businesses are a major driver of the economy and as such all levels of government have programs to develop their growth. The United States Small Business Administration has a wide variety of programs to assist small business development through various financing plans.[2]

The advantage of government sponsored programs is that the financing is relatively available, but the timing, administrative hurdles, and the amounts provided needed might be restrictive. Small businesses are also frequently able to access grants and special programs designed specifically for things like scientific research and development and export development.

---

[2]For more information see the United States Small Business Administration website https://www.sba.gov/funding-programs.

Bank Financing

Bank financing is the form of small business financing that most owners consider at some point. Bank financing can take a wide variety of forms depending on the context and needs of the business.

The two primary forms of bank financing are a term loan and an operating line of credit. A term loan is a fixed length loan with periodic interest payments. The principal of the loan can be repaid in small, regular increments, like a mortgage, or as a lump sum payment at maturity, which is called a "bullet loan." An operating line of credit is a more flexible type of loan that is intended to cover short-term needs for cash. An operating line of credit can be "drawn down" up to a preset limit, and the company only pays interest on the "drawn" amount or the amount of the line of credit that they have actually borrowed at any given point in time.

Trust receipts are a specific collateralized form of short-term bank lending that are tied to specific assets in inventory. For instance, an automobile dealer may take trust financing on each automobile that they purchase for their showroom lot. The bank providing the financing has a lien on each specific automobile that is tied to a specific trust receipt. When that automobile is sold, the bank expects repayment of that specific trust receipt. As it is a fully collateralized loan, a trust certificate is a relatively inexpensive form of financing, but the restrictions to specific assets in inventory limits its flexibility as a general financing tool.

Trade Credit

For an established business, trade credit is a frequent form of financing. Trade credit is when a supplier gives an extension on the time to pay for good or services. The advantage of trade credit is that it is a readily available way to finance for the short term the raw goods and inventory needed. The disadvantage is that it is deceptively expensive.

Trade credit is generally expressed in a form such as 3 / 10 net 50. This means that the supplier is granting the choice to the business of paying within 10 days and getting a 3 percent discount or paying the invoice in full in 50 days. At first blush it appears that the cost of this financing is simply the forgone 3 percent discount. However, it needs to be realized that the financing is only for 40 days—the difference between paying within 10 days or 50 days. When this short-term financing is annualized, its true cost is a whopping 32 percent![3]

Factoring

A major need for financing comes from the receivables of the firm. When the business extends credit, or time to pay, to its customers, this gives rise to a receivable, which is money owed to the business. To "unlock" the receivables, some businesses use a form of financing called "factoring." In factoring, the business "sells" its receivables to a financing company that specializes in financing receivables. The receivables will be sold to the factoring company at a discount, and then when the receivables are paid, the factoring company will receive the payment.

There are two general forms of factoring: with recourse and without recourse. With recourse means that if the customer does not pay their receivable within a given period of time, the factoring company will be repaid by the business that took the factor financing. Factoring without recourse means that if the customer does not pay the invoice, the factor company has no recourse to the business that factored the invoice, but instead the factor company has to deal directly with the customer to get repayment. Factoring without recourse means that the factor company is assuming the credit risk of the customer. Because of this outsourcing of credit risk, factoring without recourse is generally significantly more expensive than factoring with recourse as a source of financing.

Concluding Thoughts

In this chapter we have introduced the major financial decisions a small business manager needs to make and have begun the discussion by focusing on the financing decision. Each of the types of financial decisions outlined in this chapter exists to support the overall objective of the business. Too often, the financial decisions are the focus, rather than playing

---

[3]The formula to calculate the cost of trade credit expressed in the form of x/y Net z is $\left(1+\frac{x}{100-x}\right)^{365/z-y}-1$. For the example given in the text, this is $\left(1+\frac{3}{100-3}\right)^{365/50-10}-1=32\%$.

the supporting role that they should be playing. Ultimately, the goal of the manager should be to maximize the utility for the business owners. Financial decisions play a key role in this, but so do strategic, operational, marketing, and human resource decisions.

Obviously, how the business is financed is a key factor in its success. Too often, financing decisions are based on convenience, rather than strategically reasoned. In this chapter we attempted to highlight the main factors that should go into how a small business should be financed. Ultimately, financing decisions can have long-term implications and thus immediate needs should not necessarily take precedence. However, this is not always possible in small businesses due to the need to pivot quickly just to survive.

CHAPTER 7

Working Capital Management

In the early 2000s there was a computer commercial that showed a small group of eager young entrepreneurs sitting around a desktop computer. The leader of the group pressed the enter button to signify that the company had just gone "live" onto the Internet and into the world. Soon a ping was heard as they made their first sale. There were high fives all around the group. Soon more pings, and the entrepreneurs started to jump with glee; their company was looking like it was going to be a success. That euphoric atmosphere soon changed, however, as the flurry of pings become a torrent, and the group realized that they were swamped with orders. There was no way that they would be able to handle that demand, and thus their company was busted as quickly as it started. The theme of this commercial was obviously to sell the ad sponsor's web hosting services. The story, however, applies to many small businesses when it comes to managing their working capital. More small companies go out of business not for lack of sales, but, ironically, because they have too many sales and do not have sufficient working capital or working capital management expertise to deal with the flow.

You may be sitting there reading this as a small business operator wishing, "If only I had that problem!" Perhaps the issue is that you do have that problem, but simply have not realized it. Perhaps with better working capital management you would be able to make more in profit by selling less. If nothing else, improving working capital management can certainly help the bottom line and significantly reduce financial stress on the company (and the company's owners).

In accounting terms, working capital is frequently stated as Current Assets minus Current Liabilities. In these terms, working capital is the liquid assets of the company, or, at least conceptually, the assets net of liabilities that could be converted into cash within a year. In practical terms however, working capital management is managing the day-to-day cash flows of the company. This, to many, seems mundane compared with deciding what major projects to invest in (the subject of the next chapter) or determining the next strategic initiative for the business. However, our experience has been that working capital management is where businesses, both large and small, have their financial success created or destroyed.

There are five main tasks in working capital management; management of cash inventory, management of physical inventory, management of accounts payable, management of accounts receivable, and financing the amount of cash needed to operate the working capital management activities of the business. These five tasks are interrelated. The best way to study that interrelatedness is to examine the cash conversion cycle of the business.

Cash Conversion Cycle

To illustrate the cash conversion cycle, we will examine the operations of a very simple yet very typical business. To make things as straightforward as possible, we will assume that the company makes and sells only one type of product. For such a company, the typical product timeline will have the four following steps: (1) receive raw materials from suppliers, (2) pay suppliers for materials at some point, (3) sell the finished product, (4) receive payment from purchaser. Figure 7.1 illustrates the timeline. The key point in this timeline is that the cash goes out of the company at Step (2), and the cash comes into the company at Step (4). The other

Figure 7.1 Timeline of a typical company

thing to realize is that for the vast majority of small businesses, Step (4) occurs after Step (2). In plain language, the cash goes out before the cash comes in. The time frame between Step (2), when the cash goes out of the company, and Step (4), when the cash comes into the company, is called the Cash Conversion Cycle, or the Cash to Cash Gap.

For the vast majority of companies, the cash conversion cycle is positive in that the cash goes out before the cash goes in. There are two critical points to realize about this. The first is that it requires cash to support this cash conversion cycle and that this cash will need to be sourced and paid for. The second key point is that the larger the sales of the organization, the greater the working capital financing requirements will be. This is the key point of why many small businesses fail even though they have a large number of customers; they simply cannot keep up with the financing needs of their Cash to Cash Gap, or, equivalently, they did not understand their working capital management needs. As sales increase, the working capital needs increase, and if the working capital needs increase to the point that the working capital can no longer be financed, then the company will go bankrupt, even though they are very profitable. While it is true that the profits and the cash flows will eventually flow into the company, that does the company very little good if it must in the meantime declare insolvency.

It is relatively straightforward to calculate the Cash Conversion Cycle of the company. Consider Figure 7.2, which is Figure 7.1 redrawn with a few extra components added. The cash goes out at Step 2, when the suppliers are paid. The cash comes in at Step 4, when the purchaser pays for the product. The Cash Conversion Cycle is the time between Step 2 and Step 4.

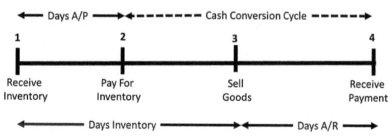

Figure 7.2 Cash conversion cycle

Now consider the time period between Step 1 and Step 2. This is the time it takes for the company to pay its suppliers. This is known as Days Account Payable. Likewise, the period between Step 1 and Step 3 is known as Days of Inventory, as it is the time period for which the company is holding inventory, whether it is raw supplies, goods in progress, or finished goods ready for sale. Then there is the time period between Step 3 and Step 4. This is the amount of time that it takes the purchaser to pay for the goods, and it is known as the Days Account Receivable.

From Figure 7.2 it should be obvious that adding up the days in the Cash Conversion Cycle to the Days Accounts Payable must be equal to the days from adding up the Days of Inventory and the Days Account Receivable. From this we get that the Cash Conversion Cycle is equal to the Days of Inventory plus the Days Account Receivable minus the Days Payable. Cash conversion cycle is shown in Equation 7.1.

$$\text{Cash Conversion Cycle} = \text{Days Inventory} + \text{Days Receivable}$$
$$- \text{Days Accounts Payable} \qquad (7.1)$$

Recalling the respective formulas from Chapter 4, we can calculate the Cash Conversion Cycle for Lake Ridge Winery for 20X3 as in Equation 7.2. The Days Inventory is 19, the Days Payable is 35, and the Days Receivable is 6, which implies that the Cash Conversion Cycle is a negative 11 days. This implies that the Lake Ridge Winery is one of very few companies that actually has a negative cash conversion cycle, which means that they receive cash before they have to pay cash out to suppliers and other expenses. The vast majority of companies will have a positive cash conversion cycle. The greater the sales, the greater the amount of working capital financing needed.

$$\text{Cash Conversion Cycle} = 365 \times \frac{42,394}{818,473} + 365 \times \frac{36,556}{2,327,412}$$
$$- 365 \times \frac{95,361}{982,168} = -11 \qquad (7.2)$$

Obviously, all else being equal, a business would like to have the Cash Conversion Cycle as small as possible. The difficulty is that all else is generally not equal, and there are trade-offs to be made in reducing the working capital needs.

There are three obvious ways to reduce the Cash Conversion Cycle: (1) reduce Days Inventory, (2) reduce Days Receivable, (3) increase Days Payable. All three methods have drawbacks, and trade-offs need to be made.

If a company reduces inventory, then customers may not see the specific product they like in stock and go to another store where they can get immediate satisfaction from their purchase. In addition to lost sales through stock-outs, a reduced level of inventory may necessitate delays in producing customer orders. We have all experienced the frustration when a part we wanted was not in stock in our local store.

The only way that a company can reduce Days Receivable is by forcing customers to pay sooner, or perhaps refusing to even extend credit for even business-to-business customers. However, there is generally a relationship between the extension of credit and the amount of sales. A reduction of credit almost always leads to a reduction in sales. Just imagine what would happen to new automobile sales if manufacturers did not make financing terms or leasing available.

Then, finally, there is the extension of Days Payable. By extending the number of days that a company takes to pay its suppliers, it risks damaging its relationships with their suppliers. In turn this means that the business may no longer get supplies shipped in a timely manner or may be limited in terms of the actual supplies that they can purchase. Taking an example from retail; many retail chains are forced to stock last year's fashions out of necessity as suppliers refuse to ship them the latest fashions unless they pay in full in advance. Having to sell out-of-date fashions exacerbates the problems for a cash-poor company.

Some businesses, depending on their industry, will have naturally high or low working capital needs. Other businesses try to set up an operating model that naturally lowers their working capital needs. Although not a small business, Wal-Mart is an excellent example of a business that is structured to have low working capital needs. To begin with, Wal-Mart has relatively few business-to-business sales that are made on credit, and thus its accounts receivable are extremely low. Secondly, Wal-Mart has always been known for its rigorous command of inventory management and the just-in-time delivery demands it makes of its suppliers. Additionally, Wal-Mart has the ability to be offered generous payment terms from its suppliers. Since it has so much market power, Wal-Mart can make demands of its suppliers that few other companies can. As a result, it is not uncommon for Wal-Mart to have a negative cash conversion cycle. That is, there are periods of time where Wal-Mart receives the cash before it has to pay the cash out. When you consider the volume of sales that Wal-Mart does, this implies that it can be hugely profitable even if it sells products at cost!

Few companies have the market dominance of Wal-Mart, and thus for the majority of companies working capital management becomes a series of trade-offs. The point is to be aware of the cash conversion cycle and of the importance of the management of it.

Cash Management

To frame the issues of cash management, consider your own personal cash management. How much cash do you like to have in your wallet or purse? This is a bit of a quaint question, so if you wish to update it, how much cash do you always like to have in your debit account? While most people cannot state a specific number, the reality is that you have an intuitive range in your mind. When your cash or debit balance is high, you are likely to feel more confident and likely to spend more freely. Conversely, when your cash or debit balance is low, you are likely to cut back on unnecessary purchases until you receive a cash inflow and your cash balance is once again above an implicit target balance.

Managing the cash balance as well as the cash target in a small business is like managing your own personal cash balance. Cash by itself has little value. It is only when cash is put to use that it creates value. However, a lack of liquidity means that opportunities may be missed and options limited. Limited liquidity can also lead to increased levels of risk and stress on both the business and the business owner.

Although cash is often called an idle asset, there are legitimate reasons for a company to hold some cash, just as there are legitimate reasons for you to have cash in your wallet or in your debit account even though it may not be earning any interest there. These reasons include transactions, risk management, funding requirements, and the flexibility and liquidity to take advantage of unexpected opportunities.

It is obvious that the organization should remain liquid enough that it can carry out the day-to-day purchases and transactions required of an ongoing business. As these transactions vary, the cash needs of the company will also vary. The objective is to have enough cash that the firm can pay its obligations on time, without having to resort to additional financing, which may be expensive. To help ease the need for excess cash balances, however, a small business will often utilize an operating line of credit that it can draw down during periods of peak transactions.

A second reason for cash balances is in terms of risk management. No matter how good the firm is at forecasting future cash needs, the reality is that operating a business is full of surprises. Having a buffer of cash allows a company to survive such surprises. Having a cash buffer also reduces stress on the company and stress on the company's owners and operators. There is a peace of mind that is involved with knowing that the next set of payroll obligations and rent obligations are covered by the cash in the company's bank accounts. This peace of mind is not a mere luxury but may actually provide management with the mental space to think of novel ways to more effectively run the business without the panic involved in racing to make a payroll deadline. While urgency tends to focus the mind, repeatedly reaching panic mode rarely produces good long-term management.

A third reason for cash balances is "compensating balances" that are required from certain funding sources. A compensating balance is a requirement that the firm maintain a minimum cash balance at all times in order for their financing to remain in good standing. Essentially, a compensating balance is like a canary in the coal mine for the financiers of the firm. A funding source wants to get its money out of the company when there are signs of trouble. A too-low cash balance is often considered to be one such sign of financial distress. Additionally, a minimum amount of net working capital (Current Assets minus Current Liabilities) may be required for similar reasons.

The final reason for cash balances is to be able to take advantage of special opportunities. Such situations might be a special purchasing opportunity or to institute a timely one-time sales promotion to take advantage of a unique set of market conditions or opportunities.

Depending on the company's ability to obtain an operating line of credit (discussed in a following section), most of the need for cash can be satisfied by utilizing the line of credit. As it is short-term financing, a line of credit is generally low cost, and in fact likely has a lower cost of financing than cash just sitting idle in a bank account. An operating line is specifically designed as a form of financing for managing the fluctuating working capital needs of companies.

There are, however, two risks to depending on a line of credit to satisfy working capital needs. The first is that the line of credit may not be available when it is most needed. For instance, if a company gets into financial difficulty, it may no longer qualify for an operating line. This was the case for many companies, both large and small, during the financial crisis of 2008. The availability of short-term financing almost totally dried up within a short time as investors and other companies (which are one of the major sources of funds for short-term lenders) hoarded their cash, which meant there were no funds available for operating lines of credit. To compound the issue, many companies were in financial distress owing to the rapid slowdown in the general economy. This made their need for short-term funding even more critical, while at the same time making them less eligible for such funding. This lack of short-term funding is why the 2008 crisis was labeled by many as a liquidity crisis. Many businesses had to shut down solely because they were dependent on short-term financing, which was no longer readily available. The second issue with short-term financing is that it tends to be quite volatile in its cost. Although short-term financing, as a general rule, is significantly less expensive than long-term financing, there are periods when its cost can rapidly spike. This will be considered when we discuss how to finance working capital in the following section.

The challenge is to balance the benefits of holding cash versus the fact that excess cash balances are an idle asset, and indeed have a cost if they need to be financed. Choosing a target cash balance is a judgment of the trade-offs from the benefits of holding cash versus the costs of excess cash. Part of making a sound judgment is forecasting cash needs. Later in this chapter we discuss the cash budget, which is an attempt to quantify the short-term cash needs of the business.

Receivables Management

Receivables management is structuring the credit policies of the firm. The elements of a receivables policy are the criteria by which credit will be extended to customers, the terms of the credit, including implied interest rate and duration of credit, and, finally, what actions will be taken when a credit customer does not or cannot pay.

The advent of credit cards and digital payments have made the receivables management of many companies much easier. Additionally, the prevalence of online shopping has also helped to accelerate electronic payments. However, particularly in business-to-business applications, there are still frequent demands for the extension of credit to customers. Not extending credit to some customers may be a deal breaker for many sales—especially large bulk sales to other businesses. This brings up the question of whom the company should grant credit to. What criteria will the company use to determine who is eligible for credit and who is not? For those that get credit, what will the terms be; will everyone get the same credit terms?

Increasing of credit availability to customers or, equivalently, liberalizing credit terms has the effect of increasing sales. However, it also increases the amount of the Accounts Receivable, and this increase needs to be financed. There is thus one benefit to Accounts Receivable (increased sales), and three costs: financing the additional Accounts Receivable, the cost and hassle of collecting late payments, and the cost of uncollectable accounts or bad debts.

Large companies can afford having staff to do a full-scale credit analysis of its customers, much like a bank would do before extending a loan. This is rarely a reasonable option, however, for a small business. A small business has neither the time nor the expertise nor the access to the necessary financial data, and therefore must turn to other sources of credit information and analysis.

To begin with, large publicly listed companies with publicly traced debt will have a public debt rating. Although not foolproof, these public debt ratings can be used—in part—to ascertain the creditworthiness of a company. For smaller companies, a creditworthiness report may be available from a mercantile agency or a credit rating agency.

A few additional guidelines can aid in the credit granting process. The first is the strength of the existing relationship. If the company has extended credit to the customer in the past, was timely payment of the receivable made? While a good payment history is not always an indication of future good payment, a history of late or partial payments can be taken as a reasonably good predictor of future problems. Experienced bankers will tell you that despite all of their sophisticated financial metrics, the character of the creditor, defined as the willingness to repay, is the most reliable indicator of credit quality. Character trumps even the capacity or the ability to repay.

Every small business owner has experienced the customer who repeatedly delays payment, argues about payment, and generally seems to find every excuse possible to avoid or drag out paying their receivable. These are all danger signs of a bad character and thus a bad credit. For accounts such as these, the small business owner has to ascertain whether the profit from the sales is worth the costs and the hassles of trying to collect from such customers.

A receivables database is a useful tool to keep track of the payment history of clients as well as of the overall trend of receivables payment times for the company. A receivables payment time that has a discernable upward trend may be an indicator that clients are having a more difficult time paying, which could be an indicator of business slowdown or an increase in uncollectable receivables.

If the decision is made to extend credit, then the credit terms need to be established. Credit terms are generally stated as $X\%/Y$ Days Net Z Days. This nomenclature means that the customer gets an $X\%$ discount if they pay within Y days, but otherwise they need to pay the invoice in full within Z days. For instance, a company may offer its clients terms of 5/10 Net 40. This means that the customer gets a 5 percent discount if they pay within 10 days, but otherwise they must pay the full amount of the invoice within 40 days. In effect, the company has extended "free" credit for 10 days and then extended an additional 30 days of credit at some implied cost for a total of 40 days of credit.

This form of credit, known as trade credit, may appear to be a low-cost form of credit, but the terms are deceiving. A naïve analysis would imply that the cost of the trade financing in the above example is 5 percent. This grossly underestimates the true cost of the credit. Consider the following analysis. If the customer pays within 10 days, they get a 5 percent discount, which means that the effective cost of their purchase is $0.95 per $1.00 of credit granted. The interest "paid" is thus $0.05. Note, however, that the period of credit is only the 30 days between day 10 and day 40. Therefore, the interest is 5 percent, for a 30-day loan period. To make this comparable to a bank loan, we need to annualize, realizing that there are 365/30, or over 12 such periods in a year for the interest to compound. The calculation of cost of trade credit is shown in Equation 7.3.

$$\left(1+\frac{0.05}{0.95}\right)^{\left(365/30\right)}-1=86.65\% \qquad (7.3)$$

As the calculation shows, the true cost of the trade credit in this example is not 5 percent, but a whopping 86.65 percent. As a rule, trade credit tends to be one of the most expensive forms of financing. It is great if you are the one extending the credit (and the clients are paying you back on time), but it is a very expensive form of financing to use for your business.

An often-forgotten step to extending trade credit is deciding what to do if the customer is late in paying, or, for whatever reason, does not pay. Often a credit notice reminding the customer of the delinquency may be enough to secure payment. But if that does not work, then the options become more limited.

Repeated attempts, letters, and phone calls may be necessary, but after a period of time these may have limited effect. They also require significant time and energy of the business trying to collect. Offers of extending the credit further with new payment terms may help, but, again, it may be just delaying the inevitable. Another alternative is to turn the debt over to a collection agency. A collection agency will generally employ increasingly aggressive tactics in order to collect on the delinquent debt. Such tactics are likely to destroy any relationship the business had with the customer, but, then again, if the customer cannot, or will not pay, they are not really a customer that one should consider keeping. Collection agencies can be effective, but they do tend to be costly. The final option is to go to court, but this again is costly with no guarantee of success.

In the final analysis, it may just be that the customer is going bank-rupt, in which case all of the businesses that extended credit will become creditors and receive whatever proceeds are available upon the liquidation of the assets of the customer.

The point about credit analysis is to consider the issues in advance and to have a policy in place. Credit policies are not something that should be developed on an ad hoc basis when a credit crisis occurs.

Cash Forecast

The cash forecast, also frequently called a cash budget, is an attempt to forecast the future cash needs of the business. It is key in determining the target cash balance, as well as forecasting short-term borrowing needs and developing a strategy for longer-term financing. The cash forecast shows the expected cash inflows as well as outflows on a monthly (or perhaps weekly, or even daily in some cases) basis for the company for a period of usually two to five years.

Figure 7.3 illustrates a hypothetical cash forecast for a typical small business.

In a cash forecast, the sources of cash are calculated as well as the uses of cash. More importantly, the timing of the cash inflows and the tim-ing of the cash outflows are calculated so a running cash balance can be determined.

The timing of the respective cash flows is key. It shows when there will be periods of excess cash, as well as periods for when there will be a need to draw upon external sources of cash, such as an operating line. In addition, the cash forecast illustrates the peak needs for external cash, which in turn allows for better planning and sourcing of necessary exter-nal financing.

In the example in Figure 7.3, note that for month four through month eight the cash balance falls below $100,000. If the company had a target cash balance of $100,000, it implies that they would require a secondary source of ready cash, such as an operating line of credit, in order to make up the difference.

The cash forecast is a very simple yet powerful tool for managing the business. It can help in planning and in assessing both cash and financing

	Month 1	Month 2	Month 3	Month 4	Month 5	Month 6	Month 7	Month 8	Month 9	Month 10	Month 11	Month 12
Beginning cash	3,300,000	$256,902	$137,820	$117,212	$95,848	$83,592	$67,651	$52,358	$80,797	$104,888	$116,434	$115,712
Sources of Cash												
Cash sales	24,840	33,120	41,400	49,680	66,240	74,520	91,080	115,920	91,080	78,660	74,520	86,940
Accounts receivable collected		6,210	8,280	10,350	12,420	16,560	18,630	22,770	28,980	22,770	19,665	18,630
Total cash available	$3,324,840	$296,232	$187,500	$177,242	$174,508	$174,672	$177,361	$191,048	$200,857	$206,318	$210,619	$221,282
Uses of Cash												
Purchases	-$50,000	-$21,150	-$25,380	-$33,840	-$38,070	-$46,530	-$59,220	-$46,530	-$40,185	-$38,070	-$44,415	-$20,000
Labour & Wages	-7,938	-10,583	-13,229	-15,875	-21,167	-23,813	-29,104	-37,042	-29,104	-25,136	-23,813	-27,782
Repairs & Maintenance		-500	-500	-500	-500	-500	-500	-500	-500	-500	-500	-500
Selling & administrative	-10,000	-10,000	-15,000	-15,000	-15,000	-20,000	-20,000	-10,000	-10,000	-10,000	-10,000	-10,000
Asset purchases	-3,000,000	-100,000										
Loan Payments		-16,179	-16,179	-16,179	-16,179	-16,179	-16,179	-16,179	-16,179	-16,179	-16,179	-16,179
Total uses of cash	-$3,067,938	-$158,412	-$70,288	-$81,394	-$90,916	-$107,022	-$125,003	-$110,251	-$95,968	-$89,884	-$94,907	-$74,461
Closing Cash Position	$256,902	$137,820	$117,212	$95,848	$83,592	$67,651	$52,358	$80,797	$104,888	$116,434	$115,712	$146,822

Figure 7.3 Sample cash forecast

needs. Also, by examining deviations of actual results from the plan numbers, an assessment of how well the business is operating can be made. The deviations from the plan, both in terms of deviations from expectations in cash inflows and deviations from expectations in cash outflows, are a useful guide to areas of improvement in producing better results.

Financing Working Capital

Working capital, like all capital, needs to be financed in some way. The general rule of thumb is to finance working capital with short-term financing and to finance long-term capital budgeting projects with longer-term financing.

There are a variety of ways to finance short-term working capital. Each of the various forms of short-term financing have advantages and disadvantages. Factors to consider when assessing the various forms of short-term financing are the ease and speed at which one can access the credit, the availability of the financing, its cost, and the flexibility or lack of flexibility implicit in the financing.

The most obvious, and most frequently used, form of short-term credit is retained earnings of the firm itself. A self-financed firm, however, may be limiting itself in terms of its growth rate. Although being self-financed is the easiest in terms of administrative hassle, it may have a high cost in terms of limited amounts that put a cap on growth, and it may not be available when most needed. Self-financing also limits the financing contacts of the company. It is almost inevitable that the company will need external financing at some time. Developing a positive credit history through external short-term financing is one way to make those external financing contacts for when they are needed.

We discussed trade credit previously in this chapter. The advantages of trade credit are that it is generally easy to obtain and generally readily available, but the disadvantage is that it also tends to be quite costly. It is generally better to use external sources of financing, which tend to be significantly less expensive.

An operating line of credit is a popular form of financing. In essence, an operating line is a credit facility where you pay interest only on the outstanding credit balance. In that way it is much like a personal credit card, although the financing rates are generally quite attractive. There will be an application required for approval for an operating line of credit, and, in addition, ongoing financial statements will generally need to be submitted to the financial institution. An operating line is also likely to come with conditions such as minimum cash balances kept on deposit at the banking institution that is granting the operating line. These compensating balances were noted earlier in this chapter. As previously mentioned, the minimum balances (and other loan conditions) help the bank to monitor the credit quality of the company that is utilizing the financing.

Note that a compensating balance also increases the effective interest rate on a loan. For instance, if a bank grants an operating loan of $1,000,000, at 7 percent interest, but requires that a minimum balance of $100,000 be kept on hand, then, effectively, the company at its peak is really borrowing only $900,000 of usable funds, but paying interest of 7 percent on the full $1,000,000 (assuming the loan is fully drawn down). This makes the effective interest 7.78 percent.

Factoring is another form of short-term financing. In factoring, the company sells it receivables to a special purpose factoring company. In essence, the factoring company buys the accounts receivable at a discount. If the factoring company has recourse to the company, meaning that they can demand payment from the company that sold the receivable for non-payment by the customer, then the discount will be relatively modest. However, if the factoring company does not have recourse and has to impose its own credit collection policies on the customer who is not paying, then the discount paid for the receivables will be significantly higher. If a company sells its receivables without recourse to a factoring company, then it has not only received financing, but has also put the credit risk in the ownership of the factoring company. However, factoring without recourse tends to be quite expensive.

There are also a wide variety of methods to finance inventories. One common method for high-cost pieces of inventory for sale is to use what is called a trust receipt. With a trust receipt, the company accepts financing from a lender, generally a bank, and in turn issues a trust receipt that effectively transfers ownership of the inventory to the lender until the item is sold. When the inventory is sold, the company then pays the lender, generally on the day of the sale or upon receipt of cash from the sale. Trust receipts are used for high-value inventories such as cars at an automobile dealership or specific pieces of jewelry in a jewelry store. The point is that a trust receipt is generally tied to specific inventory items, rather than a general source of financing.

The flip side of financing working capital is what to do with excess cash balances. Cash in a bank account is an idle asset, earning little to no interest. If the company continually finds itself with excess cash, cash that is above its target cash balance, then it may want to consider managing the cash more aggressively by entering into short-term investment assets. The investments should be of a liquid nature and easily accessible and not tied up for a significant period of time. If the company has continual and large amounts of excess cash, then it might want to consider other more valuable uses for the cash, such as a distribution of capital investments to expand the business.

Concluding Thoughts

Working capital management is perhaps not the most exciting part of managing a small business. However, it may be one of the most critical tasks for successful financial management. Working capital management is key for the long-term sustainable success of the business and effectively ties financial management to the day-to-day operations. As unglamorous as it is, strong working capital management can actually become a competitive advantage for a small business as it will allow the business to offer better credit terms to customers, more efficient inventory management, and better relations with suppliers.

CHAPTER 8

Capital Budgeting

Capital budgeting is deciding which investments the business should make or, in other words, what the business should spend money on. Intelligent capital budgeting is at the core of a growing company. Conversely, foolhardy capital budgeting has led companies of all sizes to ruin. Capital budgeting is the financial function that most directly affects the strategic direction of the firm, and, indeed, the capital budgeting plan and the strategic plan need to be in synch for either to be successful.

Like most strategic financial decisions, capital budgeting is one-part science and one-part art. In this chapter we will go over several well-accepted practices for deciding which investments a company should choose. However, each of the capital budgeting techniques we will cover requires a forecast of what will happen in the future. This, of course, is in keeping with the fact that finance is a forward-looking subject. However, it also means that inaccurate forecasts will produce incorrect capital budgeting decisions.

Even though it is not an exact science, an understanding of the principles and techniques of capital budgeting will go a long way toward helping the small business manager improve the value as well as the sustainability of the firm.

Introduction to Capital Budgeting Basics

Few firms can invest in all of the opportunities that are available to them. Both managerial and capital resources are limited, and this is particularly so for the small business. Thus, by necessity, capital budgeting frequently involves trading off the benefits of one capital project versus another. To assess these trade-offs, there are a number of considerations that should go into the capital budgeting decision.

Ideas Should Chase Money; Money Should Not Chase Ideas

Ideas should chase money; money should never chase ideas. This is an important concept that we have discussed before. However, we bring it forward again as negligence of this principle has probably been the cause of more capital budgeting debacles than any other factor. Simply because a business finds itself in the fortunate situation that it has excess cash availability, it does not necessarily mean that it should go chasing investments. Instead, the business should wait until it has excellent capital budgeting projects and then source the cash necessary to make the investment.

Does the Proposed Investment Fit with the Strategic Plan?

This is another concept that sounds so incredibly obvious that it should not bear mentioning. However, this factor is very much related to the previous consideration. A primary reason that firms invest in projects that do not fit with the strategic plan is that they find themselves with excess cash. Just like extra money burning a hole in the pockets of a 10-year-old outside a candy store, excess cash in a small business can create irrational desires to invest in projects that are outside the scope of the strategic plan.

It is one thing for a small business to invest in a new direction to diversify their business risk and to expand the scope of the firm, but such investments need to be done in a thoughtful and considered way, rather than solely on the basis of results of a capital budgeting analysis.

Is the Investment Necessary for Regulatory or Safety Reasons?

The techniques for capital budgeting covered in this section assume that the investments are discretionary. Investments required to be in compliance with laws and regulations or those required for safety reasons should not be considered discretionary and thus not subject to the techniques discussed in this chapter. However, if there are several alternatives that can be invested in to satisfy these necessary investments, then the techniques discussed in this chapter can help to select the most financially efficient alternative.

The Focus Is on the Value of the Business

Each of the techniques discussed has advantages and disadvantages. The preferred technique is the Net Present Value (NPV) Rule, which is based on the principle of making only investments that increase the value of the firm. We believe, and it is generally accepted practice, that increasing value is the principal capital budgeting factor. Increasing value is a disciplined way to assess and rank projects. It is consistent with growing the firm as well as maintaining its long-term financial health.

The components of value include all of the incremental cash flows involved with the capital budgeting project, the timing of those cash flows, and a discount factor to account for the riskiness of those cash flows.

Each of these components has a significant amount of uncertainty involved in its evaluation or requires a set of assumptions or estimates. For this reason, it is important to conduct sensitivity analysis to assess the implications of incorrect assumptions. Techniques for preforming sensitivity analysis will be discussed later in this chapter.

Triple Bottom Line Is Also Important

The final consideration, and one that may seem to be a contradiction of the previous point, is a concern for the Triple Bottom Line, or, as we put it in an earlier chapter, People, Planet, Profits. Although we believe value, or equivalently wealth, is important, we also believe (and encourage) that small business managers should follow their conscience in making their business decisions. One of the small business differences that we discussed in Chapter 1 was that small business managers have different objectives than their larger publicly traded cousins. Furthermore, it is our firm opinion that the goal of the small business manager is to maximize utility, which, we emphasized, might be very different from maximizing the utility of wealth.

We also believe that adhering to a Triple Bottom Line set of operating decisions does ironically add value. In the current context of business, good employees want to work for socially conscious companies, and many consumers are willing to pay a premium to be loyal customers. Doing good for the environment and for society as well as for the value of the firm are not necessarily contradictory. Conversely, there is a strong business case to be made for many small businesses to be socially and environmentally conscious in their decision making. A Triple Bottom Line attitude to capital budgeting can help to attract superior employees and customers and build customer loyalty.

As discussed in Chapter 2, it is quite difficult to make objective trade-offs between the economic benefits, environmental consequences, and societal consequences involved in a Triple Bottom Line analysis. As such, the methods discussed in the rest of this chapter do emphasize maximizing economic benefits or, more accurately, wealth. This is not to de-emphasize the other factors. It is simply a practical recognition that the other factors need to be incorporated into the decision making more by subjective intuition and personal values than by the objective measures we discuss in this chapter.

Components of Capital Budgeting Techniques

There are two main capital budgeting techniques that are relevant and commonly used in small business. They are the Payback Period and Net Present Value. For each of these techniques we need to know the cash flows of the project, the timing of the cash flows, and the risk associated with them.

For both techniques we need a forecast of the marginal net cash flows that the investment will involve. For the Payback Period, we also need a required payback time, and for the NPV Rule we need a rate to discount the cash flows through time. To illustrate how to implement each of the techniques through an example, consider the following case study.

Case Study: Dale's Coffee Tyme

Dale's coffee shop is a typical downtown coffee shop that is conveniently located in a street-facing storefront that is attached to a major office tower. The proprietor, Dale Swenson, has enjoyed a fair bit of success with his shop over the last 7 years. It sells the usual mix of pastries along with a range of both regular and specialty coffees and is a popular spot during the morning hours, and in midafternoon, but business drops off noticeably during the usual lunch hour segment. Currently, the shop has seating for 12, but there is potential to expand that seating to 28. Most of the traffic to the store is customers who simply come in to get a coffee, and perhaps a pastry, and then leave to take their purchase to their office desk or to enjoy elsewhere.

To expand the business, and to take advantage of the lunchtime lull, Dale is thinking of expanding into offering personal-sized gourmet pizzas and expanding the seating arrangements. Dale estimates that this will require an investment of $18,000 for a pizza oven and other capital equipment. It will also require an investment in upfront working capital of $4,000. Ongoing working capital, according to Dale's estimate, is 12 percent of net after-tax sales. To be conservative, Dale estimates that the pizza oven and equipment will have a salvage value after 5 years of $6,000. After talking with other lunch service operators in the area, Dale produced an estimate of the net after-tax cash flows expected from this project. These cash flow estimates are shown in Figure 8.1. Setting up the pizza offerings will likely cannibalize some sales of coffee and pastries. The estimates for the lost sales on an after-tax basis are also shown in Figure 8.1. Finally, Dale estimates that the project must have a return of at least 12 percent to cover the cost of capital for the business.

	0	1	2	3	4	5
New Cashflows		2,000	10,000	12,000	12,000	12,000
Lost Cashflows		2,500	2,500	2,500	2,500	2,500
Net Cashflows		-500	7,500	9,500	9,500	9,500
Capital Expenditures	18,000					
Salvage Value						6,000
Working Capital	600	-100	1,500	1,900	1,900	1,900
Change in Working Capital	600	-700	1,600	400	0	0
Net Cash Flows	-18,600	200	5,900	9,100	9,500	9,500

Figure 8.1   Dale's Coffee Tyme expansion project projected cash flows

The first step in conducting a capital budgeting analysis is projecting the after-tax cash flows from the project. In the example of the cash flows from Dale's Coffee Tyme shop, the cash flows have two major sources: net revenues from selling pizzas and lost revenues from coffee and pastries as customers change their food orders to pizza and as pastries and coffee are de-emphasized. Figure 8.1 shows the annual cash flows, with the simplifying assumption that the cash flows throughout the year will be recorded at year-end. As can be seen from Figure 8.1, there is an expectation that the cash flows will actually be reduced in the first year of pizza sales owing to the start-up time when the shop is renovating to accommodate the pizza sales, and owing to lost sales of existing customers. However, in years 2 through 5, sales of pizzas will pick up, and there will be positive net cash flows on an after-tax basis.

Projecting cash flows from a new project is never easy. It is partly a matter of doing research on customers and their habits, and partly a matter of intuition and also guesswork on the part of the small business manager. National chains have a large amount of customer data that they can rely on and, based on that data, can perform sophisticated data analytical techniques to predict demand and cash flows. That data is generally not available or applicable to the small business manager, and particularly not so when considering an expansion into a product extension, as is the case for Dale's Coffee Tyme.

The projected cash flows form the basis of the capital budgeting analysis. It is a classic case of "garbage in, garbage out." For this reason, it is important to perform scenario analysis on the cash flows, a topic that is covered later in this chapter.

The projected cash flows needed are the after-tax cash flows. This means the new revenues minus the new expenses (both variable cost revenues as well as fixed costs revenues), and the after-tax consequences. The tax consequences are beyond the scope of this book, but they include any tax reductions due to reduced profits from the start-up stage of the proposed project as well as any tax-depreciation allowances on the purchase of capital equipment. The tax implications might also extend to government grants or tax incentives for expansion or increased hirings that certain jurisdictions will extend to businesses to promote economic expansion.

They also require the capital expenditures that will need to be made. In the case of Dale's Coffee Tyme, this will include pizza ovens, pizza pans, other pizza cooking equipment, additional counter space, and food storage. The residual value of the capital equipment may also be an important component, and thus we included salvage value in our example. Small business owners are generally quite aware of the capital expenditures. A cash flow, however, that is not always so obvious is that of working capital.

Working capital includes items such as additional inventory, accounts receivables, and changes in accounts payable and might even include changes in the amount of cash needed to be kept on hand, for instance for making additional change for people who buy pizzas versus just coffee. Working capital is generally needed up front, and all needs are likely to grow as a function of sales, as discussed in the previous chapter. It is important to note that it is not the *amount* of working capital that is needed, but the *change* in working capital from period to period. It is the change in working capital that is the cash flow, just as revenues and expenses are cash flows.[1] Thus, the needed working capital for each year should be calculated and the change in working capital calculated separately, as shown in Figure 8.1.

It should be noted that for many projects most of the working capital will be recovered at the conclusion of the project. For instance, the inventory will be used up, the accounts receivable will be collected, the accounts payable will be paid, and in the case of Dales Coffee Tyme Shop, the cash will of course be completely recovered and used for other projects. In the calculations shown in Figure 8.1, we assumed that 80 percent of the working capital will be recovered in year 5, and thus there will be a positive cash flow to the business from this working capital recovery. Proper projection of working capital needs is one of the trickier aspects of a capital budgeting analysis. Many a capital budgeting analysis has been

---

[1] To help understand why it is only the change in working capital that is important, consider the expense of the pizza oven. The pizza oven is a fixed asset of the business and remains a fixed asset on the balance sheet of the business. However, the expenditure on the pizza oven is only used in the calculation for when it is purchased. The pizza oven is not counted as an expense for each year that it is an asset. It is thus only additions to the fixed assets or additions to the net working capital that are included in the analysis.

incorrectly implemented owing to the negligence of incorporating the needed working capital cash flows.

Once the cash flows have been determined, a capital budgeting technique should be selected. As previously mentioned, there are two main capital budgeting techniques that are commonly used in a small business context: the Payback Rule and the Net Present Value Rule.

Payback Rule

The Payback Rule for capital budgeting asks a simple question: whether or not the project will pay back the initial capital expenditure within a given time frame. To calculate the payback period, the cumulative cash flows for each year are calculated as shown in Figure 8.2.

From the analysis in Figure 8.2, we see that the payback period for Dale's Coffee Tyme project occurs sometime in year 4.[2] The decision for Dale is then whether or not the payback occurs within a reasonable time or not. To avoid bias, the appropriate time period should be selected before the analysis is done. For example, Dale might decide beforehand that if the payback occurs beyond year 3, the project should not be entered into. This selection of the payback period is obviously subjective, and it is this subjectivity that is the basis of one of the major weaknesses of the payback rule.

Net Present Value Rule

The Net Present Value (NPV) Rule is a more robust as well as conceptually correct rule for capital budgeting than the Payback Rule. The NPV Rule starts by calculating the present value of all of the cash flows

	0	1	2	3	4	5
Net Cash Flows	-18,600	200	5,900	9,100	9,500	9,500
Cumulative Cash Flows	-18,600	-18,400	-12,500	-3,400	6,100	15,600

Figure 8.2   Payback rule analysis

---

[2]A more precise estimate of the payback period can be made by taking the remaining negative cumulative cash flows after year 3 and determining the portion of the following year that it might take to recover these cash flows. In the foregoing example, this would be $\frac{3,400}{9,500} = 0.36$, and we would thus more precisely calculate the payback period as 3.36 years. As the payback rule is a relatively crude methodology, this level of precision is generally not warranted.

associated with the project. The discount rate is the cost of capital, or, more accurately, the Weighted Average Cost of Capital (WACC), which was discussed in Chapter 4.

Calculation of the NPV is shown in Equation 8.1.

$$NPV = \frac{CF_0}{(1+WACC)^0} + \frac{CF_1}{(1+WACC)^1}$$
$$+ \frac{CF_2}{(1+WACC)^2} + \frac{CF_3}{(1+WACC)^3} + ... \tag{8.1}$$

Where: CF$_i$ is the cash flow for period i
          WACC   is the Weighted Average Cost of Capital

The NPV represents the value added to the firm after accounting for the cost of capital that was used to invest in the project. Since the cost of capital for the business takes into account the risk of the business, the NPV also takes into account the risk of the project. The NPV tells how much more the value of the business will be if the project is undertaken. The NPV for Dale's Coffee Tyme project is shown in Figure 8.3.

The first row of Figure 8.3 shows the Net Cash Flows that constitute the values in the numerator for the NPV equation. The second row of Figure 8.3 is the values in the denominator of the NPV equation. The third row is the value of dividing each of the numerator terms by their respective denominator terms, and the total NPV in the final row of Figure 8.3 is the sum of all of the terms.

After calculating the NPV, the NPV Rule becomes obvious: accept all projects whose NPV is positive, and reject all projects whose NPV is negative. We see from the results in Figure 8.3 that going ahead with the project will enhance the value of Dale's Coffee Tyme shop by $4,187 and that thus the project should be accepted.

As the NPV analysis gives the value added, it can also be used to rank various projects. For instance, suppose Dale was alternatively considering converting the shop to have a sandwich offer versus the pizza offer. Owing

$$NPV = \frac{CF_0}{(1+WACC)^0} + \frac{CF_1}{(1+WACC)^1} + \frac{CF_2}{(1+WACC)^2} + \frac{CF_3}{(1+WACC)^3} + ...$$

Figure 8.3   NPV Rule analysis

	0	1	2	3	4	5
Net Cash Flows	-18,600	200	5,900	9,100	9,500	9,500
Discount Factor	1.00	1.12	1.25	1.40	1.57	1.76
Discounted Cash Flows	-18,600	179	4,703	6,477	6,037	5,391
NPV	4,187					

Figure 8.4 NPV analysis of sandwich alternative

to space constraints in the shop, only one of the alternatives can be implemented. The cash flows and NPV analysis for the sandwich alternative is shown in Figure 8.4.

The sandwich alternative has a lower initial capital investment and lower working capital needs. However, the net cash flows are also smaller. In deciding which alternative is financially best, it can be seen that the sandwich alternative generates a projected increase in value of $1,094, while the pizza alternative generates $4,187. For this reason, the pizza alternative would be preferred on the basis of wealth considerations.

It is worth noting that in the foregoing examples we forecast forward only for a period of 5 years. Obviously, companies will undertake projects that they expect, or at least hope, to last much longer than 5 years. Forecasting past 5 years can obviously be very imprecise and more of a guess than a legitimate forecast. However, it is equally true that if Dales Coffee Tyme expects to be in business for the long term, examining only the first 5 years of the conversion could be significantly understating its value.

For long-term projects, the NPV equation could be expanded to include more terms. However, if the net cash flows are expected to grow at a constant rate starting at some period of time, then the following simplified equation can be used, where R is the expected rate of growth.

$$NPV = \frac{CF_0}{(1+WACC)^0} + \frac{CF_1}{(1+WACC)^1} + \ldots$$

$$+ \frac{CF_n}{(1+WACC)^n} + \frac{\frac{CF_{n+1}}{(WACC-R)}}{(1+WACC)^n} \qquad (8.2)$$

The mathematical assumption made in Equation 8.2 (NPV equation for long-term projects) is that the cash flows will continue to grow each year at the rate R into perpetuity. Again, this is not a perfect assumption, as nothing grows forever, or even lasts forever. However, it is a decent approximation that gives more realistic results for long-dated projects.

Payback Rule versus NPV Rule

The Payback Rule is generally considered to be quite inferior to the NPV Rule for several reasons. The first reason is the subjectivity. The Payback Rule is based on a subjective and somewhat arbitrary desired payback period. The NPV Rule is much more objective because it is based on the actual cost of capital for the business.

Secondly, the Payback Rule cannot be used to rank projects. Just because a project returns the initial investment earlier does not mean that it is the better investment. The NPV Rule, however, explicitly calculates the expected change in value from undertaking the project, which is an obvious indicator on which to rank projects.

A third drawback of the Payback Rule is that it ignores projects that add great value but have a long payback period. As an exaggerated example, consider a company that has a 3-year payback period hurdle for them to accept a capital budgeting project. The initial investment is $1,000, and the cash inflows in years 1, 2, and 3, are $10 each year. According to the payback rule, this project would be rejected. However, suppose that the project was developing a wine that would reach its peak in year 4 and that in year 4 would have a cash inflow of $50,000. Obviously, that would be a project worth investing in!

As the previous example shows, the Payback Rule does not take into account any of the cash flows beyond the payback period. This is a significant conceptual drawback for a large publicly traded company because informed investors will always be looking at the long-term prospects of the firm. A small business, however, does not have a well-diversified set of shareholders who can afford to keep investing for a long period of time. The small business is often cash constrained and needs a relatively quick payback of invested cash in order to keep the business solvent. Therefore, many small businesses will at least use the Payback Rule as a secondary form of capital budgeting analysis despite its significant disadvantages.

The main disadvantage of the NPV Rule is that it is much more computationally intensive. Admittedly, the NPV Rule requires more work, and a bit more mathematics to calculate, but the necessary calculations are easily done in a spreadsheet program such as Excel, or in many accounting packages used by many small businesses. The conceptual, as well as the practical advantages of the NPV Rule are such that the small business manager who wants to expand and grow their business would be well advised to make the investment of time to become comfortable with the use of spreadsheets needed to conduct an NPV analysis.

Scenario Analysis and Sensitivity Analysis

The key component of a capital budgeting analysis is the projected cash flows. As discussed in Chapter 5, projecting cash flows for a business is not a trivial task, and this is particularly true when forecasting cash flows from a new project or an expansion. It is therefore imperative that some type of sensitivity or scenario analysis be conducted to provide more validity and confidence in the results and also as an indicator of how to most efficiently manage the capital budgeting project.

You will recall from Chapter 5 that scenario analysis is constructing a forecast based on changing a set, or combination, of variables to see what the outcome would be under an altered assumption about the values of the variables. A sensitivity analysis is changing just one variable at a time in order to see how just that one variable alone changes the outcome. Since capital budgeting is often such an important decision in the life of a small business, it is important to do both scenario analysis and sensitivity analysis.

Scenario analysis can help the manager plan for the financing needs if the cash flows are altered from the base assumptions. Note that results that are better than expected can cause just as many problems as results that are worse than expected. Better-than-expected sales, for instance, might require extra investment in working capital and in manufacturing equipment. If financing is not available, the firm might be forced to run equipment to the point of breaking or produce a substandard product. If working capital financing is not available for a greater than expected number of sales, then credit and sales policies may need to change, which might turn away customers for good. Of course, scenario analysis also helps the manager to plan for when results are not as good as expected. For results that are less than expected, losses from the project might need to be absorbed by the existing operations of the company, which in turn might put the sustainability of the business in doubt. In such case, a prudent manager might build a cash buffer or a contingency plan if such a scenario seemed likely.

Scenario planning is a way for the manager to see the range of possible results. It is generally wise to run an expected base case scenario, as well as a better-than-expected case, and a worse-than-expected case. Some managers like to conduct a "worst reasonable" case as well. This is a scenario in which everything could go wrong in the worst reasonable way. The worst case is trivial; sales are zero and expenses go to infinity. That is not really helpful for the manager. That is why there is an emphasis on the "worst reasonable."

Sometimes, the results of the scenario analysis are such that the capital budgeting project will be changed. For instance, it might be declined on the basis of scenario analysis even though the base case NPV is positive. This is because the worse-than-expected case is so negative that the business would be prudent to just not risk it. Conversely, the scenario analysis might show that the better-than-expected case is so strong that an extra effort, perhaps increased expenditures on advertising, would be justified to increase the probability of the best case occurring.

The sensitivity analysis offers a different insight. The sensitivity analysis shows which variables are the most important factors and thus which ones the manager should spend most of their effort in managing. For example, it might be that changing the variable cost assumption changes the NPV by only a quarter of a percent. However, changing the number of units sold by one percent changes the NPV by fifteen percent. If that was the result of the sensitivity analysis, then, obviously, the manager should be concerned much more with ensuring that units sold are meeting expectations than with controlling variable cost expenses.

Managers often think that they only have to conduct a sensitivity analysis, or a scenario analysis. However, both are necessary because they tell the manager different things about how the capital budgeting project might turn out.

Concluding Thoughts

Even if a company simply wants to maintain itself, it is almost certain that it will have to undertake capital budgeting projects. Few businesses can maintain themselves without replacing equipment or spending on maintaining their facilities. If it wants to grow and expand, then it almost certainly will need to do so. For this reason alone, capital budgeting is a key analytical skill of the small business manager. There are always alternatives for capital budgeting, and making intelligent choices among the alternatives is key for long-term success.

Capital budgeting projects, however, arise only infrequently. They are not part of the day-to-day tasks that the small business manager makes. Despite this, capital budgeting projects can be pivotal for a small business. Large corporations know the importance of capital budgeting projects and will thus have a portfolio of capital budgeting projects at any one time so they can diversify in order to remain successful. The small business manager does not have the luxury of being able to have a portfolio of capital budgeting projects but can make up for their limited scope by making intelligent capital budgeting decisions in part by using proper analytical techniques.

CHAPTER 9

Business Valuation

Valuing a business is one of the biggest financial decisions that many small business owners will ever have to make. Whether it is the decision to go into business by buying an existing business or to expand a business by buying or merging with a competitor or the valuation of shares for bringing in new equity partners, or to the consideration of selling a business, the valuation of a business can be a make-or-break exercise.

Despite its importance, valuing a business is as much an art as a science. Furthermore, different people, with different objectives and different viewpoints will all value a business differently. Therefore, when placing a value on a business, it is critical to understand the context of other stakeholders' valuation models and assumptions.

Business valuations are highly dependent on a few key variables. The current business environment, the expectations for the future business environment, and the synergies that may or may not be present are all key variables that, unfortunately, cannot be known with any degree of certainty.

Valuation Basics

There are three main methods for valuing a business. The primary method is the Discounted Cash Flow model, which shares a lot of commonalities with the Net Present Value method of capital budgeting, which was introduced in the previous chapter. While Discounted Cash Flow, or DCF, as it is commonly known, is the most theoretically correct valuation method, it is also the method that involves the most assumptions.

Given the need for sometimes heroic assumptions required of the DCF method, Comparable multiples methods are more frequently used in small business valuations. Comparable methods look to transaction values given to similar companies for which the valuation is known and scales those valuations for the relative size of the business that is being valued. Generally, the value is scaled according to the relative value of Earnings Before Interest, Taxes and Depreciation (EBITDA), or the value is scaled on the basis of the relative Net Income of the respective companies.

A third method of valuation, and indeed one that is often used as a base of valuations, is asset valuation. An asset valuation looks at what it would cost to replicate the business as it is.

Each of the methods of valuations has its advantages and disadvantages. The valuation methods differ in their ease of application, their robustness, their theoretical correctness, and their practicality. They will also differ in the valuations they produce, partly because of the differing assumptions that are needed to apply each method.

As stated earlier, valuation is subjective, and those valuing a company will have a different perspective on what the value should be. For instance, the seller of a business will likely have a different estimate for the future cash flows, their growth rate, as well as the underlying riskiness of the cash flows than the buyer of the business will likely have. Also, a buyer of a business will have different objectives and likely different plans for how the business should be structured and operated. Additionally, the buyer may have different advantages or synergies that they can exploit from buying the business, particularly if it is a larger corporation doing the purchasing.

Book Value

The simplest way to value a business is to examine the book value of the equity. This is the accounting value of the company as stated on the company's balance sheet. Theoretically, the total equity as displayed on the balance sheet should be the value of the company if the accounts did an accurate job of assessing the company's affairs. Sadly, however, an accurate valuation is not this easy or straightforward. Generally, the book value of the equity significantly understates the true value of the company for a variety of reasons.[1]

The first reason that book value understates the value of the firm is that it is looking only to the past and does not consider the potential for future growth. Secondly, the book value mainly accounts for the building and equipment of the business and ignores the goodwill and reputation that has been built up over the years by the existing owners. Thirdly, book value ignores risk and the uncertainty of the future prospects of the business. Finally, book value is inaccurate for valuation purposes because it relies on accrual accounting instead of cash flows.

Asset Valuation

One popular method to at least get a benchmark for valuation is to value the assets of a business. This would be the value of any land, building, and equipment of the firm. It would also include an estimate of the value of any proprietary knowledge such as patents or "secret recipes" or proprietary processes that the business had developed.

Asset valuation just by itself will understate the value of the business as it will not take into account the value of building the customer base and the reputation and goodwill of the business. To get a more accurate valuation, this goodwill must be estimated and added to the value of the more tangible assets of the business. An asset valuation is an attempt to value what it would cost to replicate the company as it currently exists.

In essence, asset valuation is often part of an analysis of whether it is easier and less expensive to buy an existing business or build a new business. It is the classic buy-or-build decision. Besides just calculating the replacement value of the existing business's assets, it is also important to consider the time and effort that it would take to build a new business. It will take not only time to build the needed facilities and achieve a sense of a learning curve, but also marketing expenses to build a customer base. The time and effort needed to build an equivalent business needs to be taken into account when conducting an asset valuation.

---

[1] The reader may recall footnote 2 in Chapter 3, where it was pointed out that the book value of Tesla was $7.5 billion but the market value of its shares trading on the stock exchange was $140.5 billion.

Within asset valuation there are two methods used to value a business—Going concern and liquidation value. The Going Concern methodology assumes the business will continue to operate and uses current values from the balance sheet to determine how much the business is worth. In a Liquidation valuation scenario, it is assumed that the business, for valuation purposes, is no longer operating and that the assets will be sold off (liquidated). Under this scenario assets are typically valued at a lot less than the fair market value. The value is based on the net cash left after the assets are sold off.

Despite its shortcomings, asset valuation is a convenient method to calculate a base value for a business. It can be used as a yardstick to determine the appropriateness of the other valuation methods outcomes.

Discounted Cash Flow

The DCF model says that the value of the firm should be equal to the net cash flows expected to the equity holders. Like the Net Present Value rule, which was covered in the previous chapter on Capital Budgeting, the DCF valuation examines the cash flows that are being generated by the firm and discounts those cash flows at an appropriate discount rate to account for the time value of money as well as the riskiness of the cash flows.

To apply the DCF methodology, the forecasted net operating cash flows of the firm are forecasted for several years, generally between 3 and 5 years. The net operating cash flows are considered to be the Earnings Before Interest and Taxes, which are them multiplied by one minus the tax rate. From this cash flow value are subtracted any net new cash flows that are needed for operations (such as any new expenditures for plant or equipment) and also any net new cash needed for additional working capital. Working capital for these purposes is defined as Accounts Receivable plus Inventory, minus Accounts Payable and minus Accrued Liabilities. Note that the owner or owners are paying themselves a significant salary that is beyond what a normal manager would be paid, that this abnormally large salary will affect the expenses of the business and its Net Operating Cash Flows. Thus, when projecting the cash flows, an adjustment should be made to account for what was an abnormally large payment to the owner–operators. The formula in Equation 9.1 summarizes the calculation of the Net Operating Cash Flows.

Net Operating Cash Flows$_i$ = Projected EBIT$_i$ × (1 − Tax Rate)
  − Additional Expenditures in Plant & Equipment$_i$
  − Additional Cash Need for Working Capital$_i$ (9.1)

For a variety of reasons, it is not practical to forecast the cash flows for much more than 3 to 5 years. However, it is obvious that the firm has value from the cash flows that extend beyond the forecast period. As an estimate of the value from the long-term cash flows, an estimate called the Terminal Value is calculated.

The Terminal Value is an estimate of the value of the Net Operating Cash Flows assuming that the business's cash flows grow at a constant rate into perpetuity. This is obviously an incorrect assumption because no business lasts forever; however, the mathematics are such that the longer dated cash flows do not contribute much to the total calculation. The formula is basically a mathematical shorthand that gives a reasonably accurate result. The Terminal Value is calculated as shown in Equation 9.2.

$$\text{Terminal Value}_n = \frac{\text{Net Operating Cash Flows}_{n+1}}{\text{WACC - Growth Rate}} \qquad (9.2)$$

The formula in Equation 9.2 provides an estimate of the value of the Net Operating Cash Flows from time period ($n + 1$) forward to infinity. It also provides the value of the cash flows as of time n. For instance, if the Net Operating Cash Flows are forecast for 4 years, then "n" would be 4. The estimate for the Net Operating Cash Flows at time ($n + 1$), or time 5, would then be used in Equation 9.2, to give the Terminal Value of the Net Operating Cash Flows as of time period 4.

Once a forecast for the Net Operating Cash Flows has been made, they need to be discounted by an appropriate discount rate. The Discount Rate in the formula is the appropriate rate given the relative riskiness or expected volatility of the cash flows. The Discount Rate is also based on the cost of funds that have been invested in the business. For this reason, the Discount Rate is often called the Weighted Average Cost of Capital, or WACC. The WACC is a weighted average of the cost of debt for the business (adjusted for the tax effects of debt financing) and the implied cost of the equity as discussed in Chapter 4.

The final component is to put the pieces together and calculate the total DCF. The general formula for the DCF valuation of the firm is given by Equation 9.3.

$$DCF = \sum_{i=1}^{n} \frac{\text{Net Operating Cash Flow}_i}{(1 + \text{WACC})^i} +$$

$$\frac{\text{Net Operating Cash Flows}_{n+1}/\text{WACC} - \text{Growth Rate}}{(1 + \text{WACC})^n} \quad (9.3)$$

It should be noted that this is closely related to the formula for the NPV Capital Budgeting Equation in the previous chapter. With the NPV formula, the value of the cash flows from a capital expenditure were valued after taking into account the capital expenditure. With the DCF formula, the value of the cash flows from purchasing a company is being evaluated.

Discounted Cash Flow Example

Forecasts have been compiled for the EBIT, Additional Expenditures for Plant and Equipment, and Additional Cash Needed for Working Capital for the next 3 years for company ABC. Starting in year 4, the Net Operating Cash Flows are expected to be $3,000,000 and to grow at a rate of 2 percent thereafter. The effective Tax Rate of the company is 20 percent, and the WACC is assumed to be 15 percent. Figure 9.1 shows a table with the calculation of the DCF value of the company.

The calculations in Figure 9.1 show that the projected value of ABC Corp. would be just above twenty million dollars. A key point to note about this valuation is that over fifteen million of this valuation, or just over seventy-five percent of the valuation comes from the Terminal Value. The Terminal Value itself is very sensitive to the growth rate assumption used. If the growth rate used in the Terminal Value is increased by just one percent from two percent to three percent, then the final valuation jumps to over twenty-one million dollars or

	1	2	3	4
EBIT	2,000,000	3,000,000	3,500,000	
EBIT X (1 - Tax Rate)	1,600,000	2,400,000	2,800,000	
Additional Expenditures for Plant and Equipment	50,000	75,000	0	
Additional Capital Needed for Working Capital	30,000	35,000	40,000	
Net Operating Cash Flows	1,520,000	2,290,000	2,760,000	3,000,000
Terminal Value				23,076,923
Divisor	1.15	1.32	1.52	1.52
Separate Term Values	1,321,739	1,731,569	1,814,745	15,173,452
Total Discounted Cash Flow	20,041,504			

Figure 9.1 DCF example

more than a six percent increase in value. This shows the sensitivity of the growth rate assumption. This is particularly troublesome as the growth rate assumption is especially difficult to accurately forecast.

If the business is relatively mature, and if the Net Operating Cash Flows are expected to grow at a constant rate, then a simplified form of the DCF can be used, as shown in Equation 9.4 (simplified discounted cash flow equation).

$$\text{Value} = \frac{\text{Expected Cash Flow Next Year}}{\text{WACC} - \text{Growth Rate}} \qquad (9.4)$$

As was seen in the DCF example, the simplified DCF valuation is particularly sensitive to the growth rate assumption. Small changes in the assumed growth rate can lead to large changes in the estimated value. For this reason, it is very important to do both scenario analysis and sensitivity analysis to determine the range of reasonable valuations as well as to ascertain which of the many assumptions being made are the most critical to the calculated value.

Comparables Method of Valuation

There are several different forms of comparables valuation. In essence, comparables valuation looks at similar companies and the valuations that have been placed on them when they were bought or sold. Although a cruder valuation method than DCF, it is easier to calculate and requires fewer assumptions.

The main type of comparables valuation is a price earnings multiple. The formula for a price earnings multiple valuation is shown in Equation 9.5.

$$\text{Value} = \frac{\text{Price}}{\text{Earnings}_{\text{Comparable Companies}}} \times \text{Earnings}_{\text{Company Being Valued}} \qquad (9.5)$$

The price paid for similar companies that have been sold, where the transaction value is known, is divided by the earnings of those companies. This provides the first term of the formula, which is frequently called the "multiple." The "multiple" is then multiplied by the earnings of the company that is being valued. This gives an estimate of the market value of the company for which the value is being calculated. The actual appraised value may then be adjusted on the basis of some specific valuation advantages and disadvantages of the company in question.

The comparables method has several advantages. The first is that it is easy to apply and does not require many assumptions. The second is that it is based on real transactions that have taken place, and thus it is a market-based assessment and not as subject to the bias of the stakeholders who are doing the evaluation. The main disadvantage is that it requires the value of comparable companies that have recently been sold, and for small companies that data may not always be available. Another disadvantage is that picking the group of comparable companies can be a subjective exercise and will greatly affect the valuation.

The comparables method is very much like the common method of pricing retail housing, where transactions of similar houses from a similar neighborhood are used to calculate an average price per square foot. Using this average price per square foot multiple, similar houses can be valued by taking this price per square foot multiple and multiplying by the square footage of the house being valued. The value so obtained will then be slightly adjusted by the particular attributes of the house being valued. For valuing houses, the multiple is price per square foot, and for valuing businesses the multiple is price divided by earnings.

There are a couple of issues to be aware of when using the comparables valuation. The first issue is that of what represents a similar business. A similar business is one that has similar risk, as represented by the level of stability of the Net Earnings or Net Operating Cash Flows, as well as similar growth opportunities. Generally, this means comparing businesses that are in the same or similar industries and serving a similar customer base. All else being equal, a business that has lower volatility of Net Earnings, or higher growth prospects, will command a higher comparables multiple and should have a higher valuation.

There are other factors that may be relevant in selecting similar businesses. These include factors such as geography, or the part of the company in which the business is located, the composition of the customer base, and even the uniqueness of the business.

Getting data on comparable transactions for small businesses can also be difficult. Firstly, the transaction data for the sale of most small businesses is kept private and confidential. Secondly, getting data for enough relevant companies in order to make a reasonable average, or to construct a reasonable range of multiples, can also be difficult. For some industries, as well as many types of professional practices, such as dental practices, these multiples are relatively well known. Also, they are generally well known for many popular types of franchises. However, for unique small businesses, the data can be more obscure.

The comparables method can also be used for metrics other than earnings. Multiples are also often based on Operating Cash Flows, EBITDA, or, sometimes, even Net Revenue. Other times they may be based on more specific business drivers, such as number of customers, number of subscribers' manufacturing capacity.

After the base comparables valuation is completed, adjustments should be made for the specifics of the business. For instance, newer than average manufacturing equipment would add to the value, and older than average equipment that needs significant investment to update would subtract from the value. Other factors might include specific patents or other competitive advantages. These other factors can significantly alter the valuation from the base comparables valuation.

Other Factors That Affect Value

We have covered the main methods of valuation. There are however a list of other factors that will affect valuation. In addition, it is important to recognize that different people will value a company quite differently, even if they make the same assumptions regarding the valuation factors and variables that were discussed in the previous sections of this chapter.

One of the major factors affecting valuation is that of control if just a partial non-controlling ownership stake is being valued versus a controlling share. The price per share or proportion of a business will be very different if that proportion being bought is 49 percent than if it is 51 percent. Having clear control of a business is worth a lot of value. This is particularly true in a small business where there are a few owners. With a few ownership partners, personality issues and differences of opinion over the best strategy for the business are likely to arise. In such instances, there is a lot of value in having control. This extra value is called a control premium. The majority owner, assuming they have a clear majority, and not simply the largest proportion of ownership, will be able to have veto power. This leaves the other shareholders at a distinct disadvantage when it comes to decision making. It also implies that the value of the shares for the noncontrolling shareholders will be worth significantly less on a proportional basis.

Another factor is the role of key personnel. For instance, if the success of the business is based largely on the expertise, or even just the personal brand of an existing owner or even employee, then the value of the business will be dramatically changed if that person is not part of the transfer of ownership. This is why large companies make a large part of the takeover value of a small business contingent on the key personnel staying with the larger company for a specific period of time so any knowledge or personal branding can be transferred to the new owners.

In a related manner, the value of a business being sold will be affected by how "turnkey" the business is. If the business relies on specific expertise that takes time to learn or develop, this will also affect the valuation. This is what franchise-based companies work so hard on. These franchise companies develop processes and systems that make it as easy as possible for a new owner to easily step in and operate the franchise business as quickly and as efficiently as possible. This is what makes a franchise much more attractive and much more valuable to a potential purchaser.

The liquidity of the business also matters. In other words, how hard will it be to sell the business or bring in additional shareholders. The harder it is perceived to be to sell the business in the future, the lower the valuation will be, all else being equal.

The competitive advantage of a business is a key factor in valuation in many ways. How easy it is for new competitors to enter and how much competition already exists for the business are factors that affect the valuation directly, but also indirectly by affecting the growth prospects as well as the perceived risk of the business. High barriers to entry because of reputation, cost of getting new customers, or technology will all increase the value of a business. Location can also be a competitive factor. For some types of business, location can be everything, so having the building as part of the sale, or at least having long-term lease agreements in place, can significantly improve values.

Finally, it is obvious that economic conditions will also affect the valuation. Economic conditions affect both the forecasts for growth, the perceived riskiness of the cash flows, the riskiness of the business in general, and the payback period expected for the new owners. A business in a strong operating position with strong and stable cash flows, located geographically with a strong and stable economy, will bring much more value than a similar business in an economically depressed or uncertain business environment.

Why Different People Value Companies Differently

The final aspect of valuation is to recognize that different stakeholders will come up with different valuations depending on their different viewpoints, biases, and ways of examining the business as a full or partial purchase.

The obvious difference in valuation will be between the potential buyers of the business and the sellers. Buyers will obviously overstate the growth potential and understate the risks, while the potential buyers will do the opposite. There are other factors, however, beyond the obvious biases toward valuation. The current owners will have a much better estimate of the future value, or at least a better knowledge of the value if the business remains under their control and management. The current owners essentially have inside information that goes well beyond the data that is in the financial statements. The current owners also have an impression of subtle changes in the relative changes in growth prospects and risks of the business. Potential buyers know this and will thus build in a discount in the negotiations to account for the information asymmetry.

Different potential buyers will also have different valuations based on any planned changes they have in mind if they are successful in buying the business. As in most negotiated sales, it is best if one can have more than one interested potential buyer in order to drive the negotiated price upward. Some buyers may, in fact, be willing to pay beyond true stand-alone value based on specific synergies or strategic advantages they can exploit if successful in the purchase.

If the company is being valued in order to do an initial public offering of shares, the timing of the offering and the context of other recent initial public offerings can significantly bias public sentiment toward the valuation of the shares. In the current context of social media-based company valuations and initial public offerings, the valuations methods discussed in this chapter seem quaint and significantly outdated. Ultimately, however, the price of anything is what someone is willing to pay, and what someone is willing to pay does not often follow the logic or rationality of even the best of models and forecasts.

The key point is to always remember that value is in the eye of the beholder. When valuing a business for a transaction, it is always very wise to understand the assumptions, biases, and motivations of the seller as well as of all of the potential buyers. No one has a monopoly on valuation, and no single valuation model is best in all valuations.

Concluding Thoughts

Valuation is a critically important financial task. It generally involves a critical turning point of a business, whether that is the expansion of the business by buying or merging with another business or selling the business so the owners can retire or taking the company public in an initial share offering so the business can greatly expand its scope of operations. It would be nice if there was a simple and easy-to-apply process for valuation. The reality is that valuation is as much an art as it is a science. Hopefully, this chapter has provided a guide to assist with both the science and the art of this critical and exciting financial task.

CHAPTER 10

Risk Management

What Is Risk and Risk Management

If you ask most people what their definition of risk is, you are likely to get a response along the following lines: "Risk is the possibility that something bad happens." That is the way that risk is portrayed in most media, and it is the way that many business professionals think. We believe, and theory backs us up on this, that a better definition of risk is "the possibility that bad or good things may happen." This definition allows for a much more holistic view of risk, and, as we shall soon discuss, a much better way to think about and implement risk management.

Our definition of risk involves three components. The first component of risk is that risk is about the future. The second component is that there is an element of uncertainty associated with risk. The third, and perhaps surprising, component of risk is that there is both a downside and an upside to risk. Let's briefly deal with each of the components separately.

Risk management is fundamentally about the future. Unfortunately, we cannot change the past, and the only thing we can manage for is the future. Although we look to the past for some clues about risk, the reality is that the past is relevant for risk management only to the extent that the future is likely to be the same as the past. In most industries today, the pace of change is too great to expect that the future is going to be much like the past. Unfortunately, many businesses focus on the mistakes of the past and, in doing so, not only miss the pitfalls that they will be falling into but also the opportunities that they will inevitably be exposed to.

While we cannot predict the future, we can, with a forward-looking focus, improve our ability to build an intuition about it and thus be better able to manage for it. As we cannot predict the future, it requires us to be creative. This creativity also requires us to try to be aware of our biases. Small business owners tend to be either overly optimistic or overly pessimistic when it comes to thinking of the future. Particularly for start-ups, most entrepreneurs are well aware of the survival rates for new companies, yet despite these odds they still forge ahead in the belief that their business smarts and their business ideas will allow them to be one of the exceptions. That irrational optimism is what makes economies grow and prosper.

The forward component of risk requires that we develop the skill to learn the relevant lessons from the past but to manage in the present, in order to succeed in the future. It is a skill that can be easily learned, but one needs to be aware of it, and attempt to adapt it whenever applicable.

The second component of risk management is uncertainty. There are two aspects to uncertainty; there is an aspect of probability in that if we toss a coin we know that there is a 50 percent probability that it will turn up heads, and a corresponding 50 percent probability that it will turn up tails. In addition to this, there is a set of outcomes for which we do not have probabilities in that we will have risk situations that will occur that we cannot even conceive of at the present time. That is, there are future outcomes that are impossible to even conceive of at the present time. For instance, even as late as 2015, few could conceive that Apple iTunes and the ubiquitous Apple iPod would become obsolete because of the proliferation of streaming music services.

When he was Secretary of Defense in the George W. Bush administration, Donald Rumsfeld was widely ridiculed for his comment that "there are known knowns, known unknowns, and unknown unknowns."[1]

---

[1] The full quote, which is worth reading and taking the time to understand, is: "Reports that say that something hasn't happened are always interesting to me, because as we know, there are known knowns; there are things we know we know. We also know there are known unknowns; that is to say we know there are some things we do not know. But there are also unknown unknowns—the ones we don't know we don't know. And if one looks throughout the history of our country and other free countries, it is the latter category that tend to be the difficult ones." Source: Wikipedia. n.d. "There Are Known Knowns." https://en.wikipedia.org/wiki/There_are_known_knowns, (accessed February 5, 2020).

Although it might have seemed a funny statement to the layperson, to the risk manager it was actually a very well-thought-out and insightful comment. There basically are three types of uncertainties—those that we know about, those that we know that we don't know about, and those that we don't know that we don't know about. The reality is that the small business manager needs to manage for all three types of uncertainty.

The third component of risk is that it has an upside and a downside component to it. You have probably heard various people state that the Chinese term for risk is actually a combination of risk and opportunity. The upside of risk goes hand in hand with the downside of risk. The uncertain future could turn out to be negative, and it could also equally turn out to be positive. Just managing the downside means that one is missing the opportunity to use risk management to also manage the upside opportunities. The tools and techniques for managing the downside can also be used to equal effect for seizing the upside. All it requires is an easy shift in attitude toward risk; a shift that has the potential to improve outcomes dramatically.

Briefly, before concluding this section, it is useful to examine another commonly accepted definition of risk, namely, that risk is the chance that the company will not achieve its expected outcomes. Notice that this definition of risk is consistent with ours in that the company could overachieve its expected outcomes as well as underachieve. Risk is truly a two-sided reality.

What Is Risk Management?

This brings us to the question of what is risk management? If risk is the possibility that bad or good things may happen, then this automatically implies that risk management is managing so as to decrease the probability and magnitude of bad risk events occurring, while at the same time managing so as to increase the probability and magnitude of good risk events happening.

It seems too obvious that business managers want to increase the upside. However, it is rarely thought of as a risk management exercise. Furthermore, we have found that one of the best ways to do so is to focus on the upside as well as on the downside when doing risk management. It is one of the few instances in business where one gets to have their cake and eat it too—all with the frosting on top as a bonus.

The inherent optimism of entrepreneurs and many small business managers is just as required for effective risk management as is a cautious and skeptical attitude. An extreme focus on the downside can be just as ineffective and dangerous as extreme and unwarranted optimism. The mindset to fully concentrate on both sides of risk is not difficult to do, but it is difficult to break away from old habits of thinking. That is why it is so effective to have a systematic way of thinking about, analyzing, and acting on issues and decisions regarding risk management.

The Criticality of Risk Management for Small Business

You will recall from Chapter 1 that one of the distinct differences between a small business and a large corporation is the lack of diversification. A large corporation will generally have several lines of business that provide diversification that acts as a natural risk management attribute. When one business line is suffering, it is likely that one or more business lines are doing well. This diversification helps to even things out in terms of the variability of cash flows and of profits.

The diversification, however, extends well beyond product lines. Large corporations will also be more diversified in their geographic bases as well as in their customer bases. This diversification will even out the extreme highs and the extreme lows. If one part of the business is underperforming, then it is likely that at least one or more other parts of the business are doing well and vice-versa. This natural risk management is a significant risk management advantage for the large corporation. However, it is admittedly tempered by a lack of focus that can creep into their operations.

Furthermore, a large corporation will have more resources in terms of not only financial resources but also people. More people in an organization means more ideas and a better ability to create, research, and develop diversifying products. It also means more eyes and different mindsets looking out over the horizon to see obstacles and opportunities, which is a key component of risk management. The flip side of this is that a bureaucratic mindset can creep into the large corporation as well.

A small business may have only a few product lines and may be over-committed to a limited set of business ideas and strategies. A key to risk management is to balance the focus with a mindset that is always thinking in terms of potential diversification of products, ideas, and ways of conducting business; for instance, geographical expansion or developing new sales channels such as online sales or new distributors or agents.

Two advantages that small businesses have in risk management is their closeness to their markets and their nimbleness. Small businesses are not bureaucracies and tend to be much closer to their customers and their markets than large corporations. This gives the small business manager the advantage of observing changing trends and evolving risks in a timelier fashion. Along with this advantage is the possibility of acting quickly and nimbly. Creating a risk management focus attunes the small business manager to evolving risks and allows them to exploit this valuable risk management advantage. However, this advantage will rarely be exercised if the small business is not consciously thinking with a risk management mindset.

Types of Risk

There are a plethora of risks that a small firm faces. It is sometimes helpful to classify the risks to make the job of risk management more streamlined and easier to handle. Although there are many different ways to classify risks, they can generally be grouped into the following buckets:

- Strategic Risk
- Financial Risk
- Credit Risk
- Operational Risk
- Cyber Risk
- Legal and Regulatory Risk
- Reputational Risk

Strategic risk is the risk that the strategy chosen, and the operational tactics chosen, does not lead to the expected or desired business outcomes. As a simple example, the company may have chosen a low-price strategy, although a differentiation strategy may have been preferable. Likewise, the distribution strategy or the geographical strategy may not produce the desired results. Examining strategy and operational tactics in a risk management framework can prove to be a key advantage of implementing risk management.

Financial risk is risks associated with the financial strategy of the firm. It is dependent on the financing sources used as well as the amount of financing utilized for various initiatives. As previously discussed, a general rule with financial risk is that the greater the risk in the operation of the company, the lower the financial risk should be. It should also go without saying that the greater the financial risk of the firm, the greater the need for effective risk management.

Credit risk refers to the credit policies of the firm. As discussed in Chapter 7, managing the working capital cycle, as well as the accounts receivables of the firm, is a critical function for ensuring the survival of the small firm.

Operating risk refers to the people and the processes of the firm. Accidents happen and employees as well as managers of the firm are not infallible. This also extends to stakeholders and business partners. Operating risk entails examining the functions of the firm and supply chain as well as downstream operations to ensure that they are operating as intended.

In the modern business environment, cyber risk is omnipresent. Cyber risk includes managing not only the digital footprint of the firm, but also its social media as well as its systems. It is an oft quoted saying that there are only two types of firms—those that have been hacked and those that do not realize that they have been hacked. Cyber risk is going to only continue to grow in importance as new forms of malware, ransomware, customer data hacking and threats yet to be thought of emerge from the minds of cybercriminals.

Legal and regulatory risk refers to whether the business is exposed to a lawsuit or compliance issues. Environmental risk, which is an increasingly more significant risk, can be thought of as a legal and regulatory risk as well as a reputational risk.

Last, but certainly not least, is reputational risk. Many small businesses thrive or die based on their reputation. It is a critical element of business success, but one that can change for the better or for the worse very quickly and dramatically. Social media has not only created the element of cyber risk, but has also dramatically changed the importance, impact, and management of reputational risk.

Steps in Risk Management

There are many frameworks available for risk management. Our approach for small business is to keep it simple, practical, and focused on the business. Too many organizations make risk management a bureaucracy unto itself. In such cases, risk management becomes an exercise that becomes a burden rather than an aid to business success.

There are a few central elements to a successful risk management program. They are as follows:

- Set clear and practical objectives for the risk management function
- Identify the risks
- Assess and prioritize the risks
- Choose a set of management strategies and tactics for each of the key risks
- Communicate both the risks and the rationale behind the risk management strategy to all relevant stakeholders
- Continually reevaluate and update the risk management activities, including this list.

Set Clear and Practical Risk Management Objectives

Risk management begins with being clear about not only the objectives of the firm, but also what it is hoped to achieve by practicing risk management. Risk management needs to serve the strategic and operating objectives of the company. If risk managing is not serving these overall objectives, then it has little to no value and, sadly, is likely to be destroying value. In fact, we believe that risk management, strategic management, and management are all tied into an inseparable whole. In other words, we believe that you cannot separate risk management from strategic management, and the day-to-day management functions from each other. They are the same function. Unfortunately, risk management is often thought of as an afterthought, if at all.

It is important to revisit the strategic and operating objectives of the firm when starting to build the risk management program. Every risk management initiative and activity should be helping the company to ultimately achieve these business objectives; otherwise, the risk management activity should be considered superfluous.

It is also important to clearly set out what the objectives of the risk management program by itself are going to be. There are many possible objectives for risk management. As already discussed, the primary one should be to increase the probability and magnitude of good events happening and to decrease the probability and severity of bad risk events happening. However, there are other possible objectives (and benefits) to risk management.

One frequent objective of risk management is to satisfy stakeholders. Indeed, this is where most companies start with risk management. For instance, risk management might be a requirement of a financing stakeholder such as a bank or a private investor. Risk management for this objective, however, is frequently only focused on downside risk. This is particularly true for debt holders. Debt holders ultimately do not care about how successful the firm is as long as they get their debt repaid on time. Thus, risk management for this purpose is seldom completely effective, nor is it especially efficient.

Likewise, risk management is often done to satisfy regulators. Like creditors, regulators are generally focused on downside risk. It is additionally important to realize that regulators are concerned about risk from their point of view alone. As a rule, regulators do not care about the fortunes of the business per se. The implication of this is that the risk rules that are set in place for regulatory reasons are seldom risk tactics that will improve the prospects of the firm. Indeed, much of the risk management done solely for risk management purposes is a drag on the business in terms of both cost and operating flexibility. Too frequently we have seen business, both large and small, that believe that they have effective risk management solely on the basis of the fact that they satisfy regulatory concerns. This is a very dangerous and ineffective way to consider risk management.

Whenever possible, it is useful to look for ways of putting in place risk practices for stakeholders, creditors, and regulators in a manner that they will also mesh with, and complement, the risk management that is done for the firm's objectives. However, it must be borne in mind that external stakeholders have very different risk management objectives that are generally not aligned with the risk management objectives of the business.

Another key objective for risk management is to provide peace of mind for the business owner and the business managers. This peace of mind allows the management team to focus on the business at hand, rather than worrying about the uncertainty of the business. While uncertainty will always be present, knowing that the firm has done all that it can to be well positioned for risk affords the freedom to focus on building the business.

A poor objective for risk management is to eliminate risk. Firstly, it is not possible to eliminate risk. Without risk, there is no profit. Secondly, a business exists for taking risk—albeit prudent risks. That is the function of a business.

Finally, it is important not to become complacent only because the firm is doing a good job of risk management. There is a well-known phenomenon known as risk homeostasis, which basically means that people and firms tend to forget about risk when they believe that they are safe or immune from it. For instance, the statistics show that you are more likely to be in an automobile accident if you are driving a large SUV with the latest safety systems than if you are in an older econo-box car that has bald tires. The reason is that you will take more risks, for instance go out into a hazardous snow and ice storm if you believe that the SUV will protect you regardless of the conditions.[2] It is important to not get complacent about risk simply because the business has implemented state-of-the-art risk management practices and processes. Risk is always evolving and changing, and only a conscious and continuous risk awareness will keep a business risk efficient.

---

[2]For more examples of the effect of risk homeostasis, see R. Nason. 2017. *Rethinking Risk Management: Critically Examining Old Ideas and New Concepts* (New York, NY: Business Experts Press).

Identify the Risks (The First Law of Risk Management)

The first law of risk management is "the mere fact that you acknowledge that a risk exists automatically improves your ability to manage it." Simply knowing that a risk exists implies that you will increase the probability and magnitude of it occurring if it is a good risk, as well as automatically decrease the probability and severity of it occurring if it is a bad risk. This sounds incredibly trite, but in our experience, it has repeatedly been a truism of business and of risk management.

The risks can be recorded in a risk register or, as described in the next section, in a risk map. The important thing at this stage is to become aware of as many risks as possible. Identifying risks is not a trivial task. It requires an understanding not only of the past, but also of how the future may unfold. Having a risk log for major events (again, remembering to log positive as well as negative events) helps, but, essentially, risk is a forward-looking exercise. It is easy to succumb to bias and or tunnel vision when considering the various risks. Many companies spend considerable resources on having frequent risk workshops in which they bring together a variety of stakeholders of the firm, all of whom have different perspectives and areas of expertise. By having a diversified group develop a risk analysis, a more realistic and comprehensive set of risks is likely to be developed. The better the set of risks identified, the better and more efficiently the risk management function can operate.

Assess the Risks

A key tool for assessing risks is a risk map. A risk map plots the risk along two axes. The horizontal axis measures the impact of the risk (both good risk and bad risk), while the vertical axis indicates the probability of the risk occurring. The size of the circle representing the risk is the assessment of how much control the business manager believes that they have over each of the risks. An example is shown in Figure 10.1.

The risk map is a key tool for organizing risks. Negative risks that have a large probability of occurring and/or a significant impact if they do occur are risks that the manager should pay attention to and develop a risk management strategy for. An example would be the risk labeled "A" on the left-hand side of Figure 10.1. Likewise, positive risks that are deemed

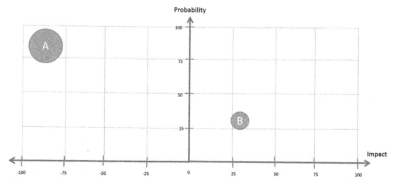

Figure 10.1   Risk map

to have a low probability of occurring and/or a small impact if they do occur should also be examined to see if there is a way that they could be made to have a greater probability of occurring and a greater impact. An example of such a risk would be the risk labeled "B" in Figure 10.1. These low-impact and low-probability positive risks are potential opportunities that the firm may not be exploiting enough.

Prioritize the Risks

After developing a risk register or a risk map and assessing the risks in terms of their impact and probability, the firm should undertake a conscious prioritization of the risks. One aspect to consider before prioritizing the risks, however, is to consider the risk appetite of the business.

The term "risk appetite" is one that is used in various ways in the risk management consulting industry. For our purposes, we define risk appetite as the overall level of risk that the company is comfortable having. A second component to this is choosing the level of each type of risk that the company is comfortable dealing with.

A company with no risk is a company that will probably not be in business for long. Companies exist to take risk, and it is their expertise in dealing with their risks that allows them to create a profit. This, again, is where it is important to remember our two-sided definition of risk: "risk is the possibility that bad or good things may happen." Eliminating risk is not a realistic choice; choosing the level of risk is. Furthermore, eliminating risk even conceptually is not a desirable choice. However, deciding on the appropriate level of risk and prioritizing the risks is a key strategic decision for managerial effectiveness.

Earlier in this chapter we listed six major classifications of risk. Risk can also be split into business risk, and financial risk, as outlined in Chapter 2, and later in Chapter 5, when we discussed the broad concept of matching financial risk to business risk. To briefly review, business risk is the expected volatility of cash flows that is independent of the choice of financing. Business risk is inherent in the industry or sector that the company is in. For instance, the restaurant industry is notorious for fluctuating cash flows, and for a wide dispersion in the expected cash flows of businesses in that industry. Conversely, a medical practice has relatively stable cash flows and, barring something unexpected happening, has very low business risk. Financial risk comes about due to the mixture of debt and equity capital used to finance the business. Businesses that have high levels of debt will have high financial risk, and their cash flows and returns will vary more widely than firms financed mainly with equity.

Thus, as a first risk prioritization, the business managers should decide on the level of business risk as well as the level of financial risk that they are willing to have as the norm. As stated in our general principles listed in Chapter 2, all else being equal, the level of financial risk should complement the level of business risk. If the business risk is high, then the norm is to have low levels of financial risk. Conversely if the business risk is low, then the managers may want to consider having higher levels of financial risk.

The second level of prioritization is to develop a risk appetite for the various sectors and the various risks discovered in the risk identification process. Some of the specific individual risks may not be considered significant to be worthy of concern. Other risks will be chosen to be strategically important risks in which the company will make it a strategic priority to become experts at managing and exploiting those risks. In between, there will be a spectrum of risk responses. (These will be discussed in the next section.)

A separate aspect of risk prioritization is to develop a risk tolerance. A risk tolerance is the set of risks that the firm has decide it simply will not accept under any circumstances. These are risks that may involve the death of an employee or the continued existence of the company. The risk tolerance may involve risks that have moral or ethical implications. In essence, the risk tolerance is a hard line on the risk appetite.

Defining how to set the risk appetite or the risk tolerance is not always trivial. In certain cases, it may be defined in terms of a dollar amount, such as the firm will not take on an obligation of more than $5 million. For other cases, however, it is trickier, particularly when there is a mixture of impact and probability. For instance, a business might reasonably say that it will not do a task that involves potential harm to an employee. However, this would preclude making deliveries, considering that driving is one of the leading causes of death. A more refined and realistic risk tolerance statement might be that the company will not undertake any activity that involves a greater than 0.5 percent chance of an employee being permanently physically harmed. Risk maps are helpful to making these distinctions.

The important point is that the choices made about risk appetite and risk tolerance should be a set of conscious choices and not a default choice. Understanding and choosing the desired level of risk is good management and leads to greater maximization of utility. Conversely, not consciously managing risk is a sign of poor management and serves as a detraction for the manager as they attempt to manage the other components of the business, as well as manage their personal stress levels.

Choose a Set of Management Strategies and Tactics for Each of the Key Risks

There are a range of possible risk responses that span the spectrum, from eliminate to ignore to embrace. Most of the time the reactions will be to enhance or to mitigate. In responding to risk, it is also important to remember that risk is two-dimensional. There is the probability factor, and there is also the impact factor. One can manage the probability factor, making the risk more or less likely to occur; or one can manage the impact factor, making the impact greater or lesser if it does indeed occur; or, finally one can risk manage on both dimensions. Additionally, there is the element of increasing the control that one believes that they have over the risk or over the control that they have of the consequences of the risk.

For those risks that are good risks, one obviously wants to increase both the likelihood of them occurring as well as the impact should they occur. Conversely for negative risks, one wants to decrease the probability as well as the impact of them occurring. Consider the risk map from Figure 10.1, redrawn as Figure 10.2. In this risk map we see two risks—Risk B, which is a positive risk, but one that is currently assessed to have a small probability of occurring and a small impact if it does occur. Conversely, we see Risk A, which is a negative risk that has been assessed as having a large probability of occurring as well as a large impact if it does occur.

In an ideal situation, actions would be taken that move the assessment of Risk B from its initial starting point to a point that indicates much greater impact and much greater probability of occurring. Likewise, in an ideal world it would be more optimal to undertake actions that move Risk A from its initial assessment position to a point with much less impact and much less probability of occurring. The reality is that not all risks can be moved in their assessment and that actions have to be undertaken to deal with the consequences of the risk.

To eliminate a given risk, one has two basic choices: outsource the risk to another entity that is able and willing to take it on, or stop the activity that is leading to the risk. For example, a business might have a product as part of its sales line that is legally dubious or has the potential for significant lawsuits, or even just harm to the reputation of the firm. Although this business line may be profitable, the assessment is that if a lawsuit were brought it would ruin the business. The business could thus opt to

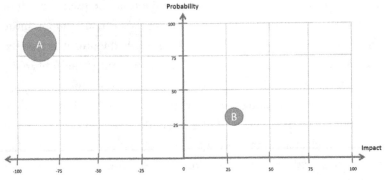

Figure 10.2 Risk map

sell this product line to another company willing to take on the risk, or it could simply cease and desist from selling the product immediately. The example of Dick's Sporting Goods deciding to no longer sell guns might be one example of such a situation. Note that a different business might decide that it is comfortable with the risk and choose to continue with the questionable product but implement risk mitigating actions such as developing a legal contingency fund, implementing stringent customer requirements, securing additional legal advice, or purchasing insurance to cover claims.

Embracing risk might entail making the risk a centerpiece of the business and developing processes and expertise to profit from the risk. For example, a company that specializes in hazardous waste clean-up has specifically made this choice and centered its business around a risk that most companies want to avoid even at high cost.

The management actions about risk will obviously vary depending on the type of risk and the context of the business. It will also vary from business to business how they choose to manage their risks. How the risk is managed is not specifically the major point. The major point is that small businesses should have risk management as a key aspect of their management plan and not as an afterthought. Going through the list of prioritized risks creates a disciplined approach to risk that will not only greatly improve the risk management of the company, but also dramatically improve its value and probability of sustained success.

Communicate Both the Risks as Well as the Rationale Behind the Risk Management Strategy to All Relevant Stakeholders

Communication is a key component of risk management. Communication involves explaining to stakeholders what the risks are, how they are being managed, and why they are being managed the way that they are. Risk management should be thought of as simply part of operations management. Every business has a consistent way of doing things that allows them to have success. These organizational methods are taught to new employees, and good companies teach not only the "what" but also the "why" as that leads to not only understanding but also compliance. The same is true of risk procedures.

Effective communication about risks and risk policies also helps to create a positive risk culture. A positive risk culture is one that has a healthy attitude toward risk and understands its two-sided nature. A positive risk culture is not one that sees risk policies as a set of "thou shall not!" but instead as a set of "how to do it better" suggestions. A positive risk culture is one that recognizes that risk surprises (both good and bad) will occur and does not consider well-intentioned mistakes or risk accidents as instances that must be punished, but instead uses them as learning opportunities for the organization.

Risk training should be a standard part of the training program for the firm and for its managers. Good risk management is simply good management, and even in a one-person business, the proprietor would want to keep abreast of the best thinking in management, operations, and sales. Likewise, risk management should be added to that list. In keeping with setting a positive risk culture, the risk training should focus on the positive operating benefits of good risk management, rather than the negative tone of much risk training. Furthermore, it should be obvious that risk training should go well beyond the normal compliance training.

There are several challenges of communicating the risk management efforts to stakeholders. The first is that risk management is not often well understood. The second is that many parts of risk management are considered to be highly technical. A third challenge is the vast number of risks that a firm may be exposed to. Effective risk communication boils the issues down simply and in an easily digestible form. One way to do this is a risk dashboard.

A risk dashboard takes its name from the dashboard of an automobile. A modern automobile is quite complicated yet very easy to drive largely because of its simplified dashboard. The dashboard lists the bare minimum of data needed, such as speed, odometer, fuel levels, and oil temperature. For most other things there is a "check engine" light that signals that further investigation (at the mechanics) is justified. If all of the possible components of driving a car were listed, then the information would overload the driver, and make driving a car a much trickier endeavor.

In a risk dashboard, the company should carefully and thoughtfully curate the most important risk variables that stakeholders, and most importantly managers, need to see to operate the business on a day-to-day basis. Also, these variables should be ones that can be easily measured or obtained. Less important, or more slowly changing risk variables, can then be checked on a periodic basis as their volatility and importance justify. The risk dashboard should contain timely updates. Many firms will update their dashboards daily, or increasingly given that the capabilities of data will have their dashboards run in real time.

There are two simple yet valuable elements of a business having a risk dashboard. The first is that it forces the managers to carefully think about what the important elements of risk are. Secondly, the constant presence keeps risk management at the forefront of management's attention. Remembering the first law of risk management (the mere fact that you acknowledge that a risk exists automatically improves your management of it), it is easy to see why the risk dashboard is a key risk management tool.

Perhaps one of the best benefits of having a process for communicating risk, such as a risk dashboard, or a regular risk report, is that it allows all stakeholders to see trends in risk developing. This allows for proactive management of risk, which is almost always better than a reactive, or even worse crisis reaction to risk.

Continually Reevaluate and Update the Risk Management Activities, Including this List

Risk by its nature is dynamic. Therefore, a risk management plan also needs to be dynamic. Each of the steps for risk management should be periodically updated, and current risk management implementations should be checked to assure that they are effectively and efficiently achieving their objectives.

The creation of the risk map, including risk identification as well as assessment, should be done at least periodically. When doing so it is especially telling to note which new risks have emerged and how the existing risks have changed their position on the risk map. The new risks, of course, will need to be prioritized, while examining the changes in the position of existing risks on the risk map will give an indication of how effective the risk management strategy is. The effectiveness of the risk management plan should also be checked against its costs, both the explicit costs in terms of expenses incurred and the implicit costs in terms of workers' hours to implement. Efficiency in risk management should be just as demanded as efficiency in manufacturing or sales. Unless periodically assessed for efficiency and effectiveness, risk management plans have a tendency to grow until they become burdensome risk bureaucracies.

Like most aspects of items related to financial management, it is the trend that matters almost as much as the actual level. The trend of the risks of a company is a telling sign of how intelligent the business is about its risk management.

Premortem and Postmortem Analysis

When a negative risk occurs, it is natural to perform a postmortem and examine what went wrong in order to prevent the same sad fate from happening again. However, just as a postmortem is useful for assessing and learning from bad risk events, they can also be used for the same purpose for assessment and learning from good risk events. Postmortems are just as effective for good risk events as they are for bad risk events. Is it not rational to want to learn from good risk events so you can increase the probability and impact of them occurring, just as you want to learn about bad risk events so you can decrease the probability and severity of them reoccurring? Thus, the next time there is a positive risk occurrence, perform a postmortem just as you would for a bad risk occurrence. You might be pleasantly surprised by what you learn. Risk really is two-sided, and upside risk should be treated just the same as downside risk for maximum risk management efficiency.

A premortem is similar to a postmortem except that it is forward looking. In a premortem you look forward and assume that the business has failed to reach its stated objectives. The premortem is a thought exercise in which you try to uncover the reasons or create the story or scenarios as to why the business objectives were not achieved. This is simply another tactic or tool for identifying risks. Again, it can be used to identify good risks as well as bad risks. In a "good risk" premortem, you might assume that the business results were much better than expected and then try to think of how that better than expected performance could come about. Your results are the good risks that might be considered for "positive" risk management.

A premortem is generally much more effective than a postmortem. A postmortem is backward looking and only looks at one specific set of circumstances. Looking backward is a very limiting way of management because you cannot change the past. A premortem, however, is forward looking and allows for proactive management. Furthermore, a premortem looks at a whole set of potential scenarios. It is a much more creative exercise and leads to more creative and likely more effective management ideas.

The interesting thing is that a "positive" premortem is generally a natural part of any strategic plan. While formulating a strategic plan, a business manager will set up their goals and objectives and naturally think of what has to happen in order for them to achieve their goals. That is effectively a premortem. While postmortems are useful, and indeed needed, premortems are likely a more effective tool for risk management.

Concluding Thoughts

It may seem as though there is a lot to think about in terms of risk management. In relation to all of the other tasks of the small business manager, it may seem that risk management would take over and not allow the manager any time to manage the other aspects of the business. This is most certainly not our intent, nor do we believe that risk management should dominate the other aspects of running a small business. We are well aware that small businesses have resource constraints, their especially in respect of management time.

We believe, however, that if risk management is integrated into the management of the firm, then it becomes a natural extension of the daily tasks that the business manager implements. In essence, good risk management is simply good management, and good management is simply good risk management. Put another way, risk management can perhaps most easily be implemented by simply doing all management tasks with a risk lens. This includes thinking about the possibility of bad and good things happening; thinking about how to increase the probability and magnitude of good things happening, while also thinking about how to decrease the probability and severity of bad risk happening.

The typical small business does not have the luxury of excess resources to deal with risks or unexpected surprises. It is therefore imperative that risk management be a core of the activities of a small business. Risk management should not be a huge resource hog, but a properly implemented risk management plan does have the potential to dramatically improve outcomes. Small businesses may not have the ample resources of their larger publicly traded relatives, but proper risk management can allow the small business to respond proactively to risks and take advantage of the nimbleness that their size provides. In this way, risk management creates a competitive advantage for small business.

About the Authors

Rick Nason, PhD, CFA

As an international consultant and founding partner with RSD Solutions Inc., Rick has advised and developed programs on valuation, risk measurement, enterprise risk management, and financial strategy since 2002. He is a frequent commentator for the media on issues related to risk management, investments, and finance in general.

Rick's reputation as a practitioner has been earned by holding multiple senior capital markets roles at a number of major international banks; he is also an award-winning academic who has developed finance courses for MBAs and executive development programs. Rick has authored many academic and professional articles and is coauthor of the textbook *Financial Management: Theory and Practice*, now in its third Canadian edition (Brigham et al. 2016).

Rick has a BSc in math and chemistry from McMurry University, an MSc in physics from the University of Pittsburgh, and an MBA and PhD from the Richard Ivey School of Business at the University of Western Ontario. He is also a CFA (chartered financial analyst) charter holder.

Dan Nordqvist, CPA, CMA, MBA, MSc

Over the last number of years Dan has developed significant expertise in corporate finance, financial analysis, and business decision support through work with a leading telecommunications corporation along with advising a wide variety of small businesses. Dan also has experience owning and operating a real estate company as well as an accounting and consulting firm. He is a senior manager with Baker Tilly Nova Scotia, where he heads up the cloud accounting team.

Dan completed his MBA and MSc both from Dalhousie University and is a chartered professional accountant. During his time at Dalhousie University and continuing to the present day, he has assisted with courses such as derivatives and risk management, corporate finance, and strategy. He has held numerous board positions and is currently the treasurer of the Better Business Bureau of the Atlantic Provinces.

Index

OTHER TITLES FROM THE FINANCE AND FINANCIAL MANAGEMENT COLLECTION

John Doukas, *Editor*

Concise and Applied Business Books

The Collection listed above is one of 30 business subject collections that Business Expert Press has grown to make BEP a premiere publisher of print and digital books. Our concise and applied books are for...

- Professionals and Practitioners
- Faculty who adopt our books for courses
- Librarians who know that BEP's Digital Libraries are a unique way to offer students ebooks to download, not restricted with any digital rights management
- Executive Training Course Leaders
- Business Seminar Organizers

Business Expert Press books are for anyone who needs to dig deeper on business ideas, goals, and solutions to everyday problems. Whether one print book, one ebook, or buying a digital library of 110 ebooks, we remain the affordable and smart way to be business smart. For more information, please visit **www.businessexpertpress.com**, or contact **sales@businessexpertpress.com**

CPSIA information can be obtained
at www.ICGtesting.com
Printed in the USA
BVHW050053301021
620268BV00008B/235